The Escape from Hunger and Premature Death, 1700–2100

Nobel laureate Robert Fogel's compelling new study examines health, nutrition, and technology over the past three centuries and beyond. Throughout most of human history, chronic malnutrition has been the norm. During the past three centuries, however, a synergy between improvements in productive technology and human physiology has enabled humans to more than double their average longevity and to increase their average body size by more than 50 percent. Larger, healthier humans have contributed to the acceleration of economic growth and technological change, resulting in reduced economic inequality, declining hours of work, and a corresponding increase in leisure time. Increased longevity has also brought increased demand for health care. Professor Fogel argues that health care should be viewed as the growth industry of the twenty-first century and that systems of financing it should be reformed. His book will be essential reading for all those interested in economics, demography, history, and health care policy.

Robert William Fogel won the Nobel Prize for Economics in 1993. He is the Charles R. Walgreen Distinguished Service Professor of American Institutions at the Graduate School of Business and Director of the Center for Population Economics at the University of Chicago. His numerous publications include *Time on the Cross: The Economics of American Negro Slavery* (with Stanley L. Engerman) and *The Fourth Great Awakening and the Future of Egalitarianism*.

D1213332

Advance praise for *The Escape from Hunger and Premature Death*

"In his usual comprehensive and perceptive way, Professor Fogel has assembled and synthesized a vast set of data which bring out the radical transformation of human health and longevity. He has set this work in the context of general economic growth and has shown the inadequacy of the usual measures of growth. He also calls attention to the changes in the economic system implied by the growing importance of health expenditures and their benefits."

> – Kenneth J. Arrow, Professor Emeritus of Economics, Stanford University

"If economic history is to fulfill the promise inherent in its subject matter, it must add the dimension of time to economics. Bob Fogel's pathbreaking study does just that and in doing so not only revises our understanding of the past but provides a thoughtful guide to policy in the future."

> – Douglass C. North, Spencer T. Olin Professor in Arts and Sciences, Department of Economics, Washington University in St. Louis

"This brief and engaging volume is sweeping in scope yet rich in detail. In it, Fogel offers an original and provocative interpretation of changes in nutrition, health, economic growth, and our daily activities, drawing on two decades of his historical research to create a distinctive vision of our future."

> – Ronald Lee, Professor of Demography and Economics, University of California at Berkeley

"For more than four decades, Professor Fogel has painstakingly unearthed evidence on the various conditions of human suffering, and on the pathways by which people have been able to emerge out of their suffering. This book, the result of many years of labor, explains Europe's escape from hunger and malnutrition in the modern era. The findings have enormous implications for regions where people have not yet been able to escape. This is social science at its noblest and best."

> – Sir Partha Dasgupta, Frank Ramsey Professor of Economics, University of Cambridge

Cambridge Studies in Population, Economy and Society in Past Time

Series Editors

RICHARD SMITH
Cambridge Group for the History of Population and Social Structure

JAN DE VRIES
University of California at Berkeley

PAUL JOHNSON
London School of Economics and Political Science

KEITH WRIGHTSON
Yale University

Recent work in social, economic, and demographic history has revealed much that was previously obscure about societal stability and change in the past. It has also suggested that crossing the conventional boundaries between these branches of history can be very rewarding.

This series exemplifies the value of interdisciplinary work of this kind and includes books on topics such as family, kinship, and neighborhood; welfare provision and social control; work and leisure; migration; urban growth; and legal structures and procedures, as well as more familiar matters. It demonstrates that, for example, anthropology and economics have become as close intellectual neighbors to history as have political philosophy or biography.

For a full list of titles in the series, please see the end of book.

The Escape from Hunger and Premature Death, 1700–2100

EUROPE, AMERICA, AND THE THIRD WORLD

Robert William Fogel
The University of Chicago and
National Bureau of Economic Research

CAMBRIDGE
UNIVERSITY PRESS

CAMBRIDGE UNIVERSITY PRESS
Cambridge, New York, Melbourne, Madrid, Cape Town, Singapore, São Paulo

Cambridge University Press
32 Avenue of the Americas, New York, NY 10013-2473, USA
www.cambridge.org
Information on this title: www.cambridge.org/9780521808781

First published 2004
Reprinted 2004, 2006

Printed in the United States of America

A catalog record for this publication is available from the British Library.

ISBN-13 978-0-521-80878-1 hardback
ISBN-10 0-521-80878-2 hardback

ISBN-13 978-0-521-00488-6 paperback
ISBN-10 0-521-00488-8 paperback

To

Sir Tony Wrigley

and to the memory of D. Gale Johnson and Peter Laslett,

whose works have greatly influenced my approach to

many of the issues discussed in this volume.

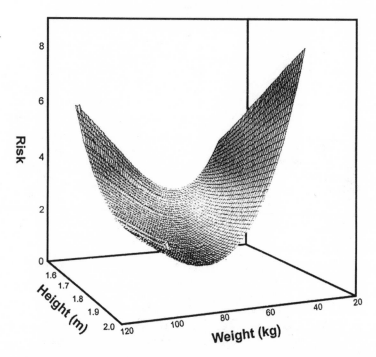

This three-dimensional diagram, called a "Waaler surface," illustrates how height and weight are related to the risk of both poor health and mortality. Its nature and uses are explained in nontechnical language in Chapter 2. Waaler surfaces were first proposed by Hans Waaler (National Institute of Public Health, Oslo) in 1984 and realized by John Kim (Center for Population Economics, University of Chicago) in various articles written or published in the late 1980s and early 1990s. Constructed by Grigoriy Abramov (Center for Population Economics, University of Chicago).

Contents

Figures

Tables

Preface

The frontispiece to this volume is a mathematical representation of the relationship between human physiology and longevity. It is emblematic of the enormous advances in the health and wealth of people over the past 300 years. It is also emblematic of the vast increase in humankind's control over the environment and of the scientific, industrial, biomedical, and cultural revolutions that are the foundations for that control.

These advances are aptly described by the term "technophysio evolution," which was coined to describe the unique nature of human progress since 1700. During these three centuries there has been a fifty-fold increase in the average incomes of the peoples of the United States and Japan and comparable increases in the leading countries of Western Europe. The peoples of these countries have greatly improved their health and more than doubled their longevity.

Technophysio evolution and its implications are the central themes of this volume. The term describes the complex interaction between advances in the technology of production and improvements in human physiology. The interaction is synergistic, which means that the total effect is greater than the sum of its parts. This interaction between technological and physiological improvements has produced a form of evolution that is not only unique to humankind but unique among the 7,000 or so generations of human beings who have inhabited the earth. Although the process has been experienced only by the last ten generations of humankind, it is still ongoing. Technophysio evolution is likely not only to accelerate during the twenty-first century, but also to have a much more far-reaching impact on the poor countries of the world than it has had to date.

This book is based on the McArthur Lectures that I delivered at Cambridge University in November 1996. In those lectures I sought to summarize my own research into the synergy between improvements in productive technology and in human physiology during the past three centuries. I also sought to place that work in the context of the revolution in biodemography, including historical demography, that began shortly after World War II and has continued down to the present day.

This volume differs from the McArthur Lectures in two respects. First, I have omitted one highly technical lecture that focused on problems of measuring the contribution of various factors to improvements in nutrition, health, and longevity. Some of these issues are discussed in Chapters 2 and 3 in a manner that makes them accessible to general readers. Second, I have added two chapters.

Chapter 4 deals with the crises in financing health care and retirement brought about by increases in longevity and the rapid growth in the demand for health care services in both rich and poor nations. In this connection, I evaluate the debate over whether advances in biotechnology will save the current national health care systems, many of which are teetering on the brink of insolvency.

Chapter 5 surveys the evidence and debates bearing on the equity of health care, both within nations and internationally. Immediately after World War II, many nations sought to establish national services that would provide complete health care to everyone. More recently, public authorities have shifted their emphasis to guaranteeing "essential" health care. The distinction between universal and essential health care is evaluated, as are debates over the optimal mix of private and government components of health services. Problems of preserving equity created by an increasing reliance on the private sector are considered.

The share of health care in national incomes has been rising in both rich and poor nations. This development has created alarm among public officials and some academic analysts. The alarm is unwarranted because the rising consumption of health care is driven by popular demand. In the pages that follow, I argue that health care is the growth industry of the twenty-first century. It will promote economic growth through its demand for high-tech products, skilled personnel, and new technologies, just as electrification spurred economic growth during the first half of the twentieth century. To achieve that potential it will, however, be necessary to reform some aspects of the system of the financing of health care that are not well suited to current needs.

Acknowledgments

I am indebted to Sir Tony Wrigley, who invited me to present the McArthur Lectures and who has influenced my research since the 1960s.

It was my good fortune to have had Simon Kuznets as my principal teacher in graduate school. He introduced me to the many exciting issues on the interrelationship between population growth and economic growth.

Much of what I have reported in this volume stems from the findings of the collaborators in the program project "Early Indicators of Later Work Levels, Disease, and Death," including Dora L. Costa, Matthew E. Kahn, Chulhee Lee, Louis L. Nguyen, Clayne L. Pope, Irwin H. Rosenberg, Nevin S. Scrimshaw, Chen Song, Werner Troesken, Sven E. Wilson, Peter D. Blanck, Christine K. Cassel, Johanna T. Dwyer, Jacob J. Feldman, Joseph P. Ferrie, Roderick Floud, Kwang-sun Lee, Robert Mittendorf, Aviva S. Must, Ira M. Rutkow, James M. Tanner, James Trussell, and Larry T. Wimmer.

The research for this book was supported by grants from the National Institute on Aging, the National Science Foundation, the

Walgreen Foundation, the National Bureau of Economic Research, and the University of Chicago.

I am indebted to Jesse Ausubel, Bernard Harris, and Paul Waggoner, who read the penultimate draft and made many helpful suggestions.

I am grateful to a number of publishers and individuals for their permission to reproduce diagrams and to republish parts of my own or jointly authored work. I would like to thank John Kim for allowing me to reprint Figures 5.1 and 5.2 from his dissertation and the University of Chicago Press for permission to reprint Figures 2.3 and 2.4 from Costa and Steckel 1997. Most of pages 67–79 originally appeared in R. W. Fogel, "Economic and social structure for an ageing population," *Philosophical Transactions of the Royal Society of London*, series B, 352 (1997): 1905–17. The section "Forecasting health care costs in China and other Third World countries" in Chapter 4 is a revised version of pages 7–10 of Robert W. Fogel, "Forecasting the demand for health care in OECD nations and China," *Contemporary Economic Policy* 21 (2003): 1–10, © Western Economic Association International. Chapter 5 was published previously as Robert W. Fogel and Chulhee Lee, "Who gets health care?" *Daedalus* 131, no. 1 (2002): 107–17, © 2002 by Robert W. Fogel. I would like to thank Chulhee Lee for allowing me to use material that he coauthored in this book. Part of the Appendix originally appeared as the note to Figure 3 on p. 34 of Robert William Fogel, "New sources and new techniques for the study of secular trends in nutritional status, health, mortality, and the process of aging," *Historical Methods* 26 (1993): 5–43, © 1993 Robert W. Fogel; that note was written primarily by John Kim. Tables A2 and A3 appeared in the same article and were computed by John Kim.

Katherine A. Chavigny and Susan E. Jones bore the brunt of the editorial work on these lectures, which included not only numerous suggestions for improvements in style but also most of the work on the citations. Katharine J. Hamerton also assisted in the editorial process. Ruma Niyogi prepared the Glossary and the Biographical Notes. The various drafts were typed by Marilyn Coopersmith, Karen Brobst, and Pat Mackins-Morrow.

The drive to explain the secular decline in mortality pushed research in three directions. Initially, much of this effort revolved around the construction of time series of birth and death rates that extended as far back in time as possible in order to determine just when the decline in mortality began. Then, as data on mortality rates became increasingly available, they were analyzed in order to determine factors that might explain the decline as well as to establish patterns or laws that would make it possible to predict the future course of mortality.

Somewhat later, efforts were undertaken to determine the relationship between the food supply and mortality rates. Between the two world wars, the emerging science of nutrition focused on a series of diseases related to specific nutritional deficiencies. In 1922 shortages in vitamin D were shown to cause rickets. In 1933 thiamine deficiency was identified as the cause of beriberi, and in 1937 inadequate niacin was shown to cause pellagra.[3] Although the energy required for basal metabolism (the energy needed to maintain vital functions when the body is completely at rest) had been estimated at the turn of the century, it was not until after World War II that estimates of caloric requirements for specific activities were worked out. During the three decades following World War II, research in nutritional sciences conjoined with new findings in physiology to demonstrate a previously unknown synergy between nutrition and infection and to stimulate a series of studies, still ongoing, of numerous and complex routes through which nutrition affects virtually every vital organ system.[4]

The effort to develop time series of mortality rates also took an enormous leap forward after World War II. Spurred by the development of high-speed computers, historical demographers in France and England developed new time series on mortality from baptismal and burial records that made it possible to trace changing mortality from 1541 in the case of England and from 1740 in the case of France.[5]

Two other critical sources of data became available during the 1970s and 1980s. One was food-supply estimates that were developed in France as a by-product of the effort to reconstruct the pattern of French economic growth from the beginning of the

Industrial Revolution. Once constructed, the agricultural accounts could be converted into estimates of the output of calories and other nutrients available for human consumption through a technique called "National Food Balance Sheets." Such estimates are currently available for France more or less by decade from 1785 down to the present. In Great Britain the task of reconstructing the growth of the food supply was more arduous, but estimates of the supply of food are now available by half century from 1700 to 1850 and by decade for much of the twentieth century.[6]

The other recent set of time series pertains to physique or body builds – height, weight, and other anthropometric (bodily) measures. The systematic recording of information on height was initially an aspect of the development of modern armies, which began to measure the height of recruits as early as the beginning of the eighteenth century in Sweden and Norway and the middle of the eighteenth century in Great Britain and its colonies such as those in North America. The measurement of weight did not become widespread in armies until the late 1860s, after the development of platform scales. However, there are scattered samples of weights that go back to the beginning of the nineteenth century. During the 1960s and 1970s, recognition that data on body builds were important indicators of health and mortality led to the systematic recovery of this information by economic and social historians seeking to explain the secular decline in mortality.[7]

These rich new data sources supplemented older economic time series, especially those on real wages (which began to be constructed late in the nineteenth century) and real national income (which were constructed for OECD nations mainly between 1930 and 1960). These new sources of information about human welfare, together with advances in nutritional science, physiology, demography, and economics, form the background for these chapters. Before plunging into my own analysis and interpretation of this evidence, however, I want to summarize the evolution of thought about the causes of the secular decline in mortality.

Between the late 1930s and the end of the 1960s a consensus emerged on the explanation for the secular trend. A United Nations study published in 1953 attributed the trend in mortality to four categories of advances: (1) public health reforms, (2) advances in medical knowledge and practices, (3) improved personal hygiene, and (4) rising income and standards of living. A United Nations study published in 1973 added "natural factors," such as the decline in the virulence of pathogens, as an additional explanatory category.[8]

A new phase in the effort to explain the secular decline in mortality was ushered in by Thomas McKeown, who, in a series of papers and books published between 1955 and the mid-1980s, challenged the importance of most of the factors that previously had been advanced for the first wave of the mortality decline. He was particularly skeptical of those aspects of the consensus explanation that focused primarily on changes in medical technology and public health reforms. In their place he substituted improved nutrition, but he neglected the synergism between infection and nutrition and so failed to distinguish between diet and nutrients available for cellular growth. McKeown did not make his case for nutrition directly but largely through a residual argument after having rejected other principal explanations. The debate over the McKeown thesis continued through the beginning of the 1980s.[9] However, during the 1970s and 1980s, it was overtaken by the growing debate over whether the elimination of mortality crises was the principal reason for the first wave of the mortality decline, which extended from roughly 1725 to 1825.

The systematic study of mortality crises and their possible link to famines was initiated by Jean Meuvret in 1946. Such work was carried forward in France and numerous other countries on the basis of local studies that made extensive use of parish records. By the early 1970s, scores of such studies had been published covering the period from the seventeenth through the early nineteenth centuries in England, France, Germany, Switzerland, Spain, Italy, and the Scandinavian countries. The accumulation of local studies provided the foundation for the view that mortality crises accounted for a large part of total mortality during the early modern era, and that the decline in mortality rates between the mid-eighteenth and

mid-nineteenth centuries was explained largely by the elimination of these crises, a view that won widespread if not universal
support.[10]

Only after the publication of death rates based on large representative samples of parishes for England and France did it become
possible to assess the national impact of crisis mortality on total
national mortality. Figure 1.1 displays the time series that emerged
from these studies. Analyses of these series confirmed one of the important conclusions derived from the local studies: Mortality was
far more variable before 1750 than afterward. They also revealed
that the elimination of crisis mortality, whether related to famines
or not, accounted for only a small fraction of the secular decline
in mortality rates. About 90 percent of the drop was due to the
reduction of "normal" mortality.[11]

In discussing the factors that had kept past mortality rates high,
the authors of the 1973 United Nations study of population noted
that "although chronic food shortage has probably been more
deadly to man, the effects of famines, being more spectacular, have
received greater attention in the literature."[12] Similar points were
made by several other scholars, but it was not until the publication
of the Institut national d'études démographiques data for France
and the E. A. Wrigley and R. S. Schofield data for England that
the limited influence of famines on mortality became apparent. In
chapter 9 of the Wrigley and Schofield volume, Ronald Lee demonstrated that although there was a statistically significant lagged relationship between large proportionate deviations in grain prices
and similar deviations in mortality, the net effect on mortality after
five years was negligible.[13] Similar results were reported in studies
of France and the Scandinavian countries.[14]

The current concern with the role of chronic malnutrition in
the secular decline of mortality does not represent a return to the
belief that the entire secular trend in mortality can be attributed to
a single overwhelming factor. Specialists currently working on the
problem agree that a range of factors is involved, although they
have different views on the relative importance of each factor. The
unresolved issue, therefore, is how much each of the various factors

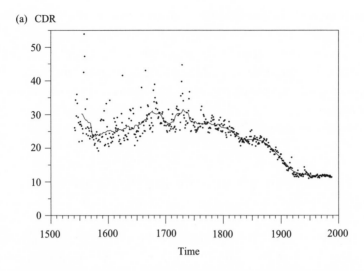

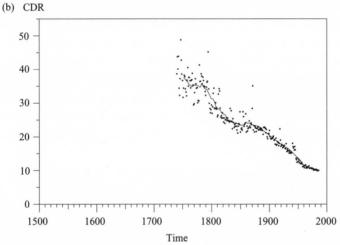

Figure 1.1 Secular Trends in Mortality Rates in England and France.
(a) England 1541–1975. (b) France 1740–1974.

Note: CDR = crude death rate, which is computed as the total deaths in a given year divided by the midyear population and multiplied by 1,000. Each diagram shows the scatter of annual death rates around a 25-year moving average. On sources and procedures, see Fogel 1992, notes to Table 9.1.

contributed to the decline. Resolution of the issue is essentially an accounting exercise of a particularly complicated nature that involves measuring not only the direct effect of particular factors but also their indirect effects and their interactions with other factors. I now consider some of the new data sources and new analytical techniques that have recently been developed to help resolve this accounting problem.[15]

The Dimensions of Misery during the Eighteenth and Nineteenth Centuries

It is now clear that although the period from the middle of the eighteenth century to the end of the nineteenth has been hailed justly as an industrial revolution, as a great transformation in social organization, and as a revolution in science, these great advances brought only modest and uneven improvements in the health, nutritional status, and longevity of the lower classes before 1890. Whatever contribution the technological and scientific advances of the eighteenth and nineteenth centuries may have made ultimately to this breakthrough, escape from hunger and high mortality did not become a reality for most ordinary people until the twentieth century.

This point can be demonstrated by looking first at the amount of food available to the typical worker in England and France during the eighteenth and early nineteenth centuries. Because at that time food constituted between 50 and 75 percent of the expenditures of laboring families, improvement in the conditions of their lives should have been evident in their diets. However, Table 1.2 shows that the energy value of the typical diet in France at the start of the eighteenth century was as low as that of Rwanda in 1965, the most malnourished nation for that year in the tables of the World Bank. England's supply of food per capita exceeded that of France by several hundred calories but was still exceedingly low by current standards. Indeed, as late as 1850, the English availability of calories hardly matched the current Indian level.

Table 1.2 Secular Trends in the Daily
Caloric Supply in France and Great Britain,
1700–1989 (calories per capita)

Year	France	Great Britain
1700		2,095
1705	1,657	
1750		2,168
1785	1,848	
1800		2,237
1803–12	1,846	
1845–54	2,480	
1850		2,362
1909–13		2,857
1935–39	2,975	
1954–55	2,783	3,231
1961		3,170
1965	3,355	3,304
1989	3,465	3,149

Source: Fogel, Floud, and Harris, n.d.

The supply of food available to ordinary French and English families between 1700 and 1850 was not only meager in amount but also relatively poor in quality. In France between 1700 and 1850, for example, the share of calories from animal foods was less than half of the modern share, which is about one-third in rich nations. In 1750 about 20 percent of English caloric consumption was from animals. That figure rose to between 25 and 30 percent in 1750 and 1800, suggesting that the quality of the English diet increased more rapidly than that of the French during the eighteenth century. However, although the English were able to increase their diet in bulk, its quality subsequently diminished, with the share of calories from animals falling back to 20 percent in 1850.[16]

One implication of these low-level diets needs to be stressed: Even prime-age males had only a meager amount of energy available for work. By work I mean not only the work that gets counted in national income and product accounts (which I will call "NIPA work"), but also all activity that requires energy over and above baseline maintenance. Baseline maintenance has two components. The larger component is the basal metabolic rate (or BMR), which accounts for about four-fifths of baseline maintenance. It is the amount of energy needed to keep the heart and other vital organs functioning when the body is completely at rest. It is measured when an individual is at complete rest, about 12 to 14 hours after the last meal.[17] The other 20 percent of baseline maintenance is the energy needed to eat and digest food and for vital hygiene. It does not include the energy needed to prepare a meal or to clean the kitchen afterward.

It is important to keep in mind that not all goods and services produced in a society are included in the NIPA. When the NIPA were first designed in the early 1930s, they were intended to measure mainly goods and services traded in the market. It was, for example, recognized that many important contributions to the economy, such as the unpaid labor of housewives, would not be measured by the NIPA. However, the neglect of nonmarket activities was to a large extent made necessary by the difficulty in measuring them given the quantitative techniques of the time. Moreover, with a quarter of the labor force unemployed in 1932, Congress was most concerned about what was happening to market employment. It was also assumed that the secular trend in the ratio of market to nonmarket work was more or less stable. This last assumption turned out to be incorrect. Over time, NIPA work has become a smaller and smaller share of total activities. Furthermore, we now have the necessary techniques to provide fairly good estimates of nonmarket activities. Hence in these chapters I will attempt to estimate the energy requirements of both market and nonmarket work.

Dietary energy available for work is a residual. It is the amount of energy metabolized (chemically transformed for use by the body) during a day, less baseline maintenance. Table 1.3 shows that in rich countries today, around 1,800 to 2,600 calories of energy are available for work to an adult male aged 20–39. Note that calories for females, children, and the aged are converted into equivalent males aged 20–39, called "consuming units," to standardize the age

Table 1.3 A Comparison of Energy Available for Work Daily per Consuming Unit in France, England and Wales, and the United States, 1700–1994 (in kcal)

Year	(1) France	(2) England and Wales	(3) United States
1700		720	2,313[a]
1705	439		
1750		812	
1785	600		
1800		858	
1840			1,810
1850		1,014	
1870	1,671		
1880			2,709
1944			2,282
1975	2,136		
1980		1,793	
1994			2,620

[a] Prerevolutionary Virginia.

Source: Fogel, Floud, and Harris, n.d.

and sex distributions of each population. This means that if females aged 15–19 consume on average 0.78 of the calories consumed on average by males aged 20–39, they are considered 0.78 of a male aged 20–39, insofar as caloric consumption is concerned, or 78 percent of a consuming unit.

During the eighteenth century, France produced less than one-fifth of the current U.S. amount of energy available for work. Once again, eighteenth-century England was more prolific, providing more than a quarter of current levels, a shortfall of well over 1,000 calories per day. Only the United States provided energy for work equal to or greater than current levels during the eighteenth and early nineteenth centuries.

When interpreting Table 1.3, it should not be assumed that work actually performed on a given day was always exactly equal to the ingested energy not used for maintenance. Work on any day can exceed or fall short of the amount allowed by the residual. If actual work requirements fall short of that made possible by the residual, the unused energy will be stored in the body as fat. If actual work exceeds the residual, the body will provide the energy from fat stores or from lean body mass. Among impoverished populations today, work during busy seasons is often sustained by drawing on the body's stores of energy and then replenishing these stores during slack seasons. However, when such transactions are large, they can be a dangerous way of providing the energy needed for work. Although the body has a mechanism that tends to spare the lean mass of vital organs from such energy demands, the mechanism is less than perfect and some of the energy demands are met from vital organs, thus undermining their functioning.

Some investigators concerned with the link between chronic malnutrition and morbidity and mortality rates during the eighteenth and nineteenth centuries have focused only on the harm done to the immune system. The now famous table of nutrition-sensitive infectious diseases published in *Hunger and History* in 1983 stressed the way that some infectious diseases are exacerbated by the undermining of the immune system.[18] Unfortunately, some scholars have misinterpreted this table, assuming that only the outcome of a narrow list of so-called nutritionally sensitive infectious diseases is affected by chronic malnutrition. Both the prevalence and mortality rates of chronic diseases, such as congestive heart failure, can be affected by seriously impairing the physical functioning of the heart muscles, the lungs, the gastrointestinal tract, or some other vital organ systems other than the immune system. I will return to this issue in subsequent chapters.

An important implication of Table 1.2 needs to be made explicit. Today the typical American male in his early thirties is about 177 cm (69.7 inches) tall and weighs about 78 kg (172 pounds). Such a male requires daily about 1,794 calories for basal metabolism and a total of 2,279 calories for baseline maintenance.[19] If either the British or the French had been that large during the eighteenth century, virtually all of the energy produced by their food supplies would have been required for maintenance, and hardly any would have been available to sustain work. The relatively small

Table 1.4 Estimated Average Final Heights (cm) of Men Who Reached Maturity between 1750 and 1975 in Six European Populations, by Quarter Centuries

(1) Date of Maturity by Century and Quarter	(2) Great Britain	(3) Norway	(4) Sweden	(5) France	(6) Denmark	(7) Hungary
1. 18-III	165.9	163.9	168.1			169.1
2. 18-IV	167.9		166.7	163.0	165.7	167.2
3. 19-I	168.0		166.7	164.3	165.4	166.7
4. 19-II	171.6		168.0	165.2	166.8	166.8
5. 19-III	169.3	168.6	169.5	165.6	165.3	
6. 20-III	175.0	178.3	177.6	174.3	176.0	170.9

Sources and notes: Lines 1–5: Great Britain: all entries were computed from data in Floud, Wachter, and Gregory 1990. Norway: Floud 1984a, who cites Kiil 1939. Kiil estimated the height of recruits who were age 18.5 in 1761 at 159.5 cm, to which I added 4.4 cm to obtain the estimated final height 163.9 for 18-III. Sweden: Sandberg and Steckel 1987, Table 1. Decades straddling quarter centuries were given one-half the weight of decades fully within a quarter century. France: rows 3–5 were computed from von Meerton 1989 as amended by Weir 1993, with 0.9 cm added to allow for additional growth between age 20 and maturity (Gould 1869: 104–5; cf. Friedman 1982, p. 510 n. 14). The entry for row 2 is derived from a linear extrapolation of von Meerton's data for 1815–36 back to 1788, with 0.9 cm added for additional growth between age 20 and maturity. Denmark: the entries are from Floud 1984a, who reported data analyzed by H. C. Johansen in 1982 and communicated privately. Hungary: all entries are from Komlos 1989, Table 2.1, p. 57. *Line 6:* the entry for Great Britain is from Rona, Swan, and Altman 1978, Table 3. The entries for Norway, Sweden, and Denmark are from Chamla 1983, Tables VII, XII, and XIV. Norwegian and Swedish heights are for 1965, Danish heights are for 1964. The entries for France and Hungary are from Eveleth and Tanner 1976, p. 284 (cf. p. 277).

food supplies available to produce the national products of these two countries about 1700 suggest that the typical adult male must have been quite short and very light.

This inference is supported by data on stature and weight that have been collected for European nations. Table 1.4 provides estimates of the final heights of adult males who reached maturity between 1750 and 1975. It shows that during the eighteenth and nineteenth centuries, Europeans were severely stunted by modern standards (cf. line 6 of Table 1.4).

Table 1.5 A Comparison of the Average Daily Uses of Dietary Energy in England and Wales in 1700 and 1800 (all lines in millions of calories, except line 3)

	(1) 1800	(2) 1700	(3) 1700 Counterfactual
1. Total daily dietary energy consumed (production plus net imports)	20,509	11,470	9,718
2. Energy used to produce agricultural output	871	913	777
3. Energy productivity in agriculture (the output/input ratio of dietary energy)	20.4	12.5	12.5
4. Energy consumed in the agricultural sector	7,731	6,804	7,042
5. Energy consumed outside of the agricultural sector	12,778	4,666	2,676
6. Energy used to produce nonagricultural output	1,684	683	0

Note: The numerator of the output/input ratio in line 3 excludes imported calories. This table supersedes Table 5 in Fogel 1997.
Source: Fogel, Floud, and Harris, n.d.

Could the English and French of the eighteenth century have coped with their environment without keeping average body size well below what it is today? How Europeans of the past adapted their size to accommodate their food supply is shown by Table 1.5, which compares the average daily consumption of calories in England and Wales in 1700 and 1800 by two economic sectors: agriculture and everything else. Within each sector the estimated amount of energy required for work is also shown. Line 3 presents a measure of the efficiency of the agricultural sector in the production of dietary energy. That measure is the number of calories of food output per calorie of work input.[20]

Column 1 of the table presents the situation in 1800, when calories available for consumption were quite high by prevailing European standards (about 2,933 calories per consuming unit daily), when adult male stature made the British the tallest national population in Europe (about 168 cm or 66.1 inches at maturity) and relatively heavy by the prevailing European standards, averaging about 61.5 kg (about 136 pounds) at prime working ages, which implies a body mass index (BMI) of about 21.8. The BMI, a measure of weight standardized for height, is computed as the ratio of weight in kilograms to height in meters squared. Food was relatively abundant by the standards of 1800 because, in addition to substantial domestic production, Britain imported about 13 percent of its dietary consumption. However, as column 1 indicates, British agriculture was quite productive. English and Welsh farmers produced over 20 calories of food output (net of seeds, feed, inventory losses, etc.) for each calorie of their work input. About 44 percent of this output was consumed by the families of the agriculturalists.[21]

The balance of their dietary output, together with some food imports, was consumed by the nonagricultural sector, which constituted about 64 percent of the English population in 1801.[22] Although food consumption per capita was about 6 percent lower in this sector than in agriculture, most of the difference was explained by the greater caloric demands of agricultural labor. Food was so abundant compared to France that even the English paupers and vagrants, who accounted for about 20 percent of the population c.1800, had about three times as much energy for begging and other activities beyond maintenance as did their French counterparts.[23]

The food situation was tighter in 1700, when only about 2,724 calories were available daily per consuming unit. The adjustment to the lower food supply was made in three ways. First, the share of dietary energy made available to the nonagricultural sector in 1700 was a third lower than was the case a century later. That constraint necessarily reduced the share of the labor force of 1700 engaged outside of agriculture. Second, the amount of energy available for work per equivalent adult worker was lower in 1700 than in 1800, both inside and outside agriculture, although the shortfall was somewhat greater for nonagricultural workers. Third, the energy required for basal metabolism and maintenance was lower in 1700 than in 1800 because people were smaller. Compared with 1800, adult heights of males in 1700 were down by 3 cm, their BMI was about 21 instead of 22, and their weights were down by about

4 kg. Constriction of the average body size reduced the number of calories required for maintenance by 105 calories per consuming unit daily.

The last figure may seem rather small. However, it accounts for half of the total shortfall in daily caloric consumption.[24] That figure is large enough to sustain the proposition that variations in body size were a principal means of adjusting the population to variations in the food supply. The condition for a population to be in equilibrium with its food supply at a given level of consumption is that the labor input (measured in calories of work) is large enough to produce the requisite amount of food (also measured in calories). Moreover, a given reduction in calories required for maintenance will have a multiplied effect on the number of calories that can be made available for work in the national income sense. The multiplier is the inverse of the labor force participation rate (workers per person in the population). Since only about 35 percent of equivalent adults were in the labor force, the potential daily gain in calories for NIPA work was not 105 calories per equivalent adult worker but 300 calories per equivalent adult NIPA worker.[25]

The importance of the last point is indicated by considering columns 2 and 3 of Table 1.5. Column 2 shows that the daily total of dietary energy used for NIPA work in 1700 was 1,596 million calories, with 913 million expended in agriculture and the balance in nonagriculture. Column 3 indicates what would have happened if all the other adjustments had been made but body size remained at the 1800 level, so that maintenance requirements were unchanged. The first thing to note is that energy available for food production would have declined by 15 percent. Assuming the same input/output ratio and amount of imports, the national supply of dietary energy would have declined to 9,718 million calories, of which over 70 percent would have been consumed within the agricultural sector. The residual available for nonagriculture would not even have covered the requirements of that sector for basal metabolism, leaving zero energy for NIPA work in nonagriculture. In this example, the failure to have constrained body size would have reduced the energy for NIPA work by about 51 percent.[26]

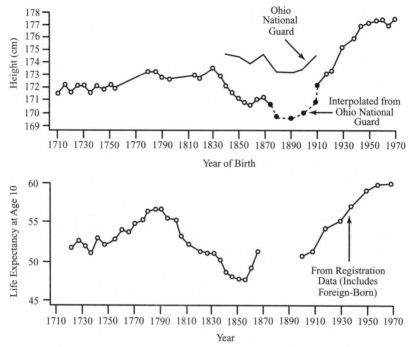

Figure 1.2 Trend in Mean Final Height of Native-Born White American Males and Trend in Their Life Expectancy at Age 10.

Sources: Fogel 1986; Costa and Steckel 1997.

Note: Height is by birth cohort, and life expectancy at age 10 is by period.

Varying body size was a universal way that the chronically malnourished populations of Europe responded to food constraints. However, even the United States, which was awash in calories compared with Europe, suffered from serious chronic malnutrition, partly because the high rate of exposure to infectious diseases prevented many of the calories that were ingested from being metabolized and partly because of the large share of dietary energy expended in NIPA work.

Figure 1.2 summarizes the available data on U.S. trends in stature (which is a sensitive indicator of the nutritional status and health of a population) and in life expectancy since 1720. Both series contain striking cycles. They both rise during most of the eighteenth century, attaining substantially greater heights and life expectancies than prevailed in England during the same period. Life expectancy began to decline during the 1790s and continued to do so for about half a century. A new rise in heights, the one with which we have long been familiar, probably began with co-horts born during the last decade of the nineteenth century and continued down to the present.[27]

Figure 1.2 reveals not only that Americans achieved modern heights by the middle of the eighteenth century, but also that they reached levels of life expectancy not attained by the general pop-ulation of England or even by the British peerage until the first quarter of the twentieth century.

Similar cycles in height appear to have occurred in Europe. For example, Swedish heights declined by 1.4 cm between the third and fourth quarters of the eighteenth century. Hungarian heights declined more sharply (2.4 cm) between the third quarter of the eighteenth century and the first quarter of the nineteenth century. There also appears to have been regular cycling in English final heights (heights at maturity) throughout the nineteenth century, al-though the amplitude of these cycles was more moderate than those of the United States or Hungary. A second height decline, which was accompanied by a rise in the infant mortality rate, occurred in Sweden during the 1840s and 1850s.[28]

This evidence of cycling in stature and mortality rates during the eighteenth and nineteenth centuries in both Europe and America is puzzling to some investigators. The overall improvement in health and longevity during this period is less than might be expected from the rapid increases in per capita income indicated by national in-come accounts for most of the countries in question. More puzzling are the decades of sharp decline in height and life expectancy, some of which occurred during eras of undeniably vigorous economic growth.[29]

The prevalence of meager diets in much of Europe, and the cy-cling of stature and mortality even in a country as bountiful in food as the United States, shows how persistent misery was down almost to the end of the nineteenth century and how diverse were the factors that prolonged misery. It is worth noting that during the 1880s Americans were slightly shorter than either the English or the Swedes, but a century earlier the Americans had had a height advantage of 5 to 6 cm over both groups. This conflict between vigorous economic growth and very limited improvements or reversals in the nutritional status and health of the majority of the population suggests that the modernization of the nineteenth century was a mixed blessing for those who lived through it. However, the industrial and scientific achievements of the nineteenth century were a precondition for the remarkable achievements of the twentieth century, including the unprecedented improvements in the conditions of life experienced by ordinary people.

2

Why the Twentieth Century
Was So Remarkable

Research during the past two decades has produced significant advances in the description and explanation of the secular decline in mortality. Although many of these findings are still tentative, they suggest a new theory of evolution that Dora Costa (an economist and biodemographer at MIT) and I call "techno-physio evolution." Studies of the causes of the reduction in mortality point to the existence of a synergism between technological and physiological improvements that has produced a form of human evolution that is biological but not genetic, rapid, culturally transmitted, and not necessarily stable.[1] This process is still ongoing in both rich and developing countries. In the course of elaborating this theory, thermodynamic and physiological aspects of economic growth will be defined, and their impact on economic growth rates will be discussed.

Unlike the genetic theory of evolution through natural selection, which applies to the whole history of life on earth, techno-physio evolution applies only to the past 300 years of *human* history and particularly to the past century.[2] Despite its limited scope, technophysio evolution appears to be relevant to forecasting likely trends over the next century or so in longevity, the age of onset of chronic diseases, body size, and the efficiency and durability of vital organ systems. It also has a bearing on such pressing issues of public policy as the growth in population, in pension costs, and in health care costs.

The theory of technophysio evolution rests on the proposition that during the past 300 years, particularly during the past century, human beings have gained an unprecedented degree of control over their environment – a degree of control so great that it sets them apart not only from all other species, but also from all previous generations of *Homo sapiens*. This new degree of control has enabled *Homo sapiens* to increase its average body size by over 50 percent and its average longevity by more than 100 percent since 1800, and to greatly improve the robustness and capacity of vital organ systems.

Figure 2.1 helps to point up how dramatic the change in the control of the environment after 1700 has been. During its first 200,000 or so years, *Homo sapiens* increased at an exceedingly slow rate. The discovery of agriculture about 11,000 years ago broke the tight constraint on the food supply imposed by a hunting and gathering technology, making it possible to release between 10 and 20 percent of the labor force from the direct production of food and also giving rise to the first cities. The new technology of food production was so superior to the old one that it was possible to support a much higher rate of population increase than had existed prior to c. 9000 B.C. Yet, as Figure 2.1 shows, the advances in the technology of food production after the *second* Agricultural Revolution (which began about A.D. 1700) were far more dramatic than the earlier breakthrough, since they permitted the population to increase at so high a rate that the line of population appears to explode, rising almost vertically. The new technological breakthroughs in manufacturing, transportation, trade, communications, energy production, leisure-time services, and medical services were in many respects even more striking than those in

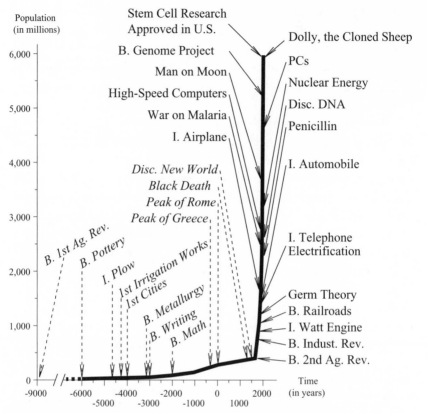

Figure 2.1 The Growth of World Population and Some Major Events in the History of Technology.

Sources: Cipolla 1974; Clark 1961; Fagan 1977; McNeill 1971; Piggott 1965; Derry and Williams 1960; Trewartha 1969. See also Allen 1992, 1994; Slicher van Bath 1963; Wrigley 1987.

Note: There is usually a lag between the invention (I) of a process or a machine and its general application to production. "Beginning" (B) usually means the earliest stage of this diffusion process.

agriculture. Figure 2.1 emphasizes the huge acceleration in both population and technological change during the twentieth century. The increase in the world's population between 1900 and 1990 was four times as great as the increase during the whole previous history of humankind.

The Relationship between Body Size and the Risk of Death at Middle and Late Ages

Although Figure 2.1 points to changes in technology that permitted a vast increase in population, it does not reveal a connection between technological changes and physiological benefits. To get at that question, we need to consider a number of recent studies that have demonstrated the predictive power of height and body mass with respect to morbidity and mortality at later ages. The results of two of these studies are summarized in Figures 2.2 and 2.3. Figure 2.2 plots the relationship between relative mortality risk and height found by Hans Waaler among Norwegian men aged 40–59 measured in the 1960s and among Union Army veterans measured at ages 23–49 and at risk between ages 55 and 75.[3] Short men, whether modern Norwegians or nineteenth-century Americans, were much more likely to die than tall men. Height

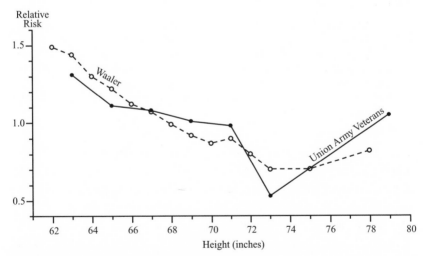

Figure 2.2 Relative Mortality Risk among Union Army Veterans and among Modern Norwegian Males.

Note: A relative risk of 1.0 means that the risk at that height was equal to the average risk of death in the entire population of males of the specified ages. Also note that the tallest data point, in both the Norwegian and Union Army cases, is not statistically significant.

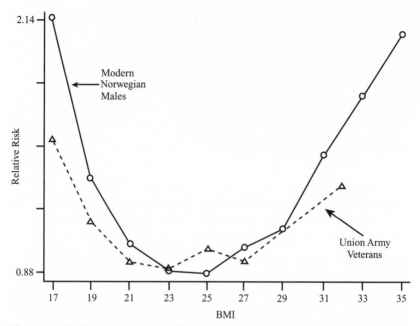

Figure 2.3 Comparison of Relative Mortality Risk by BMI among Men 50 Years of Age, Union Army Veterans around 1900 and Modern Norwegians.

Source: Reprinted from Costa and Steckel 1997, p. 54, with the permission of The University of Chicago Press. © 1997 by the National Bureau of Economic Research.

Note: In the Norwegian data, BMI for 79,084 men was measured at ages 45–49, and the period of risk was 7 years. BMI of 550 Union Army veterans was measured at ages 45–64, and the observation period was 25 years.

has also been found to be an important predictor of the relative likelihood that men aged 23–49 would have been rejected by the Union Army during 1861–65 because of chronic diseases.[4] Despite significant differences in ethnicity, environmental circumstances, the array and severity of diseases, and time, the functional relationship between height and relative risk is strikingly similar in the two cases.[5]

Waaler has also studied the relationship in Norway between body mass, measured by BMI, and the risk of death.[6] A curve summarizing his findings for men aged 45–49 is shown in Figure 2.3.

The curve for Union Army veterans measured at ages 45–64 and followed for 25 years is also shown in Figure 2.3. Among both modern Norwegians and Union Army veterans, the curve is relatively flat within the range 22–28, with the relative risk of mortality hovering close to 1.0. However, at BMIs of less than 22 and over 28, the risk of death rises quite sharply as BMI moves away from its mean value.

It is important to understand that, as used in this discussion, "risk" or "risk of death" refers to the likelihood of dying during any defined period of time; the risk period in Figure 2.4, for example, is 18 years. Mortality risk is most commonly presented as the crude death rate (CDR). In this diagram, a relative risk of 1.0 is the average risk of dying in the population as a whole over all heights and weights (i.e., the average crude death rate – the total deaths during a year divided by the midyear population). Greater or lower risks that vary with height and weight are all expressed relative to the average risk in the population as a whole. For example, a relative risk of 2.0 means having a risk that is twice the average CDR.

Although Figures 2.2 and 2.3 are revealing, they are not sufficient to shed light on the debate over whether moderate stunting impairs health when weight-for-height is adequate. To get at the "small-but-healthy" issue, one needs an iso-mortality surface that relates the risk of death to height and weight simultaneously. Such a surface is presented as a three-dimensional diagram in the frontispiece. For some purposes, it is more convenient to represent a three-dimensional surface in two dimensions, as is done in topographical maps. Such a two-dimensional surface, presented in Figure 2.4, was fitted to Waaler's data. Figure 2.4 combines three different types of curves. The solid curves are iso-mortality risk curves, each of which traces out all the combinations of height and weight that represent a given level of risk. Transecting the iso-mortality map is a set of iso-BMI curves, represented by dashed lines. Each iso-BMI curve is the locus of all of the combinations of height and weight that yield a specific level of BMI, ranging from

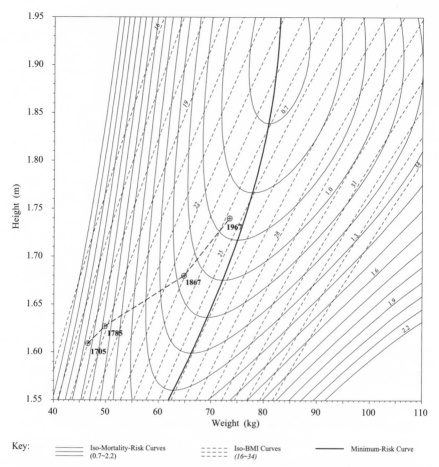

Key: ═══ Iso-Mortality-Risk Curves (0.7~2.2)   ‑ ‑ ‑ Iso-BMI Curves (16~34)   ──── Minimum-Risk Curve

Figure 2.4 Iso-Mortality Curves of Relative Risk for Height and Weight among Norwegian Males Aged 50–64, with a Plot of the Estimated French Height and Weight at Four Dates.

Sources: Data points for 1705 and 1785 are from Fogel, Floud, and Harris, n.d.; the point for 1867 is from Baxter 1875, 1: 58–59; the point for 1967 is from Eveleth and Tanner 1976.

Note: For a brief description of the procedure used to estimate the 1705 and 1785 points, see Fogel 1997; a more extensive explanation appears in Fogel, Floud, and Harris, n.d. This figure supersedes versions that have appeared previously.

16 to 34. The heavy black curve running through the minimum point of each iso-mortality curve gives the weight that minimizes risk at each height.

Figure 2.4 shows that even when body weight is maintained at what Figure 2.3 indicates is an "ideal" level (BMI = 25), short men are at substantially greater risk of death than tall men. Figure 2.4 also shows that the ideal BMI varies with height. A BMI of 25 is ideal for men in the neighborhood of 176 cm (69 inches), but for tall men the ideal BMI is between 22 and 24, while for short men (under 168 cm or 66 inches) the ideal BMI is about 26.[7]

Superimposed on Figure 2.4 are rough estimates of heights and weights in France at four dates. In 1705 the French probably achieved equilibrium with their food supply at an average height of about 161 cm (63 inches) and a BMI of about 18. Over the next 290 years the food supply expanded with sufficient rapidity to permit both the height and the weight of adult males to increase. Figure 2.4 implies that while factors associated with height and weight jointly explain virtually all of the estimated decline in French mortality rates over the period between c. 1785 and c. 1867, they explain only about 35 percent of the decline in mortality rates between c. 1867 and c. 1967.[8]

The analysis in this section points to the misleading nature of the concept of subsistence as Malthus originally used it and as it is still widely used today. Subsistence is not located at the edge of a nutritional cliff, beyond which lies demographic disaster. Rather than one level of subsistence, there are numerous levels at which a population and a food supply can be in equilibrium in the sense that they can be indefinitely sustained. However, some levels will have smaller people and higher normal mortality than others.[9]

The Relevance of Waaler Surfaces for Predicting Trends in Chronic Diseases

Poor body builds increased vulnerability to diseases, not just contagious diseases but chronic diseases as well. This point is

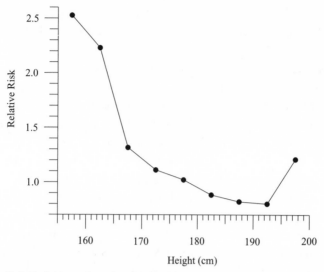

Figure 2.5 Relationship between Height and Relative Risk of Ill Health in NHIS Veterans Aged 40–59.

Source: Fogel, Costa, and Kim 1993.

Note: This curve is similar to the curve in Figure 2.2, except that Figure 2.5 gives the average risk of reporting poor health by height, whereas Figure 2.2 gives the average risk of dying by height. Also note that the tallest data point is not statistically significant.

demonstrated by Figure 2.5, which shows that chronic conditions were much more frequent among short young men than among tall men in the U.S. National Health Interview Surveys (NHIS) for 1985–88. Virtually the same functional relationship between stature and chronic diseases was found in the 1860s among young adult and middle-aged men examined by the surgeons of the Union Army. Stunting during developmental ages had a long reach and increased the likelihood that people would suffer from chronic diseases at middle and late ages.[10]

American males born during the second quarter of the nineteenth century were not only stunted by today's standards, but their BMIs at adult ages were about 10 percent lower than current U.S. levels (see Figure 2.6).[11] The difference in average BMI between adult males today and those born in the nineteenth century widened with age, perhaps because of the accumulated effects of

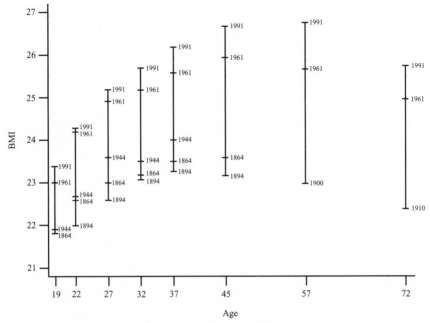

Figure 2.6 Mean BMI by Age Group and Year, 1864–1991.

Source: Reprinted from Costa and Steckel 1997, p. 55, with the permission of The University of Chicago Press. © 1997 by the National Bureau of Economic Research.

Note: The age groups are centered at the marks and are ages 18–19, 20–24, 25–29, 30–34, 35–39, 40–49, 50–64, and 65–79. For some years BMI is not available for a specific age group.

differences in nutritional intake and physical activity and because of the increased prevalence of chronic conditions at older ages (see Figure 2.6). The implication of combined stunting and low BMI is brought out in Figure 2.7, which presents a Waaler surface for morbidity estimated by John Kim (1993) from NHIS data for 1985–88 that is similar to the Norwegian surface for mortality (see Figure 2.4).

Figure 2.7 also presents the coordinates in height and BMI of Union Army veterans who were 65 or over in 1910 and of veterans (mainly of World War II) who were the same ages during 1985–88. These coordinates imply that increases in height and BMI should have led to a decline of about 35 percent in the prevalence of chronic diseases between the two cohorts.[12]

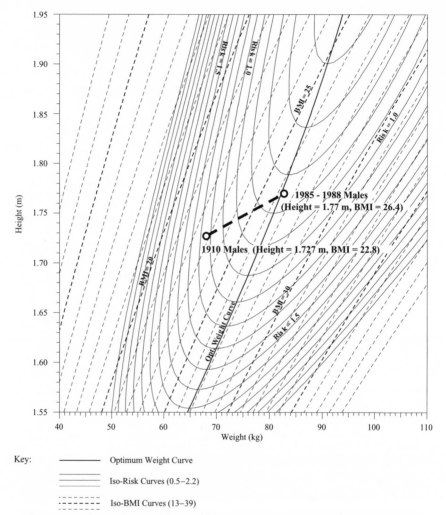

Key: ——————— Optimum Weight Curve

 Iso-Risk Curves (0.5–2.2)

 - - - - - - - Iso-BMI Curves (13–39)

Figure 2.7 Health Improvement Predicted by NHIS 1985–88 Health Surface.

Source: Kim 1993.

Note: All risks are measured relative to the average risk of morbidity (calculated over all heights and weights) among NHIS 1985–1988 white males aged 45–64.

Table 2.1 Comparison of the Prevalence of Chronic Conditions among Union Army Veterans in 1910, Veterans in 1983 (Reporting Whether They Ever Had Specific Chronic Conditions), and Veterans in NHIS, 1985–88 (Reporting Whether They Had Specific Chronic Conditions during the Preceding 12 Months), Aged 65 and Above, Percentages

Disorder	1910 Union Army Veterans	1983 Veterans	Age-Adjusted 1983 Veterans	NHIS 1985–88 Veterans
Musculoskeletal	67.7	47.9	47.2	42.5
Digestive	84.0	49.0	48.9	18.0
Hernia	34.5	27.3	26.7	6.6
Diarrhea	31.9	3.7	4.2	1.4
Genitourinary	27.3	36.3	32.3	8.9
Central nervous, endocrine, metabolic, or blood	24.2	29.9	29.1	12.6
Circulatory^a	90.1	42.9	39.9	40.0
Heart	76.0	38.5	39.9	26.6
Varicose veins	38.5	8.7	8.3	5.3
Hemorrhoids^b	44.4			7.2
Respiratory	42.2	29.8	28.1	26.5

Notes: Prevailing rate of Union Army veterans are based on examinations by physicians. Those for the 1980s are based on self-reporting. Comparison of the NHIS rates with those obtained from physicians' examinations in NHANES II indicates that the use of self-reported health conditions does not introduce a significant bias into the comparison. See Fogel, Costa, and Kim 1993 for a more detailed discussion of possible biases and their magnitudes.

^{a} Among veterans in 1983, the prevalence of all types of circulatory diseases will be under-estimated because of underreporting of hemorrhoids.

^{b} The variable indicating whether the 1983 veterans ever had hemorrhoids is unreliable.

Source: Fogel, Costa, and Kim 1993.

This exercise is consistent with what actually occurred.[13] Table 2.1 compares the prevalence of chronic diseases among Union Army men aged 65 and over in 1910 with two surveys of veterans of the same ages in the 1980s.[14] That table indicates that musculoskeletal and respiratory diseases were 1.6 times as prevalent, heart disease was 2.9 times as prevalent, and digestive diseases were 4.7 times as prevalent among veterans aged 65 or over in 1910 as in 1985–88. Young adults born between 1822 and 1845 who survived the deadly infectious diseases of childhood and adolescence were not freer of degenerative diseases than persons of the same ages today, as some have suggested, but were more afflicted. Hernia rates at ages 35–39, for example, were more than three times as high in the 1860s as in the 1980s. Of special note is the much higher incidence of clubfoot in the 1860s – a birth anomaly that suggests that the uterus was far less safe for those awaiting birth than it is today. The provisional findings thus suggest that chronic conditions were far more prevalent throughout the life cycle for those who reached age 65 before World War I than is suggested by the theory of the epidemiological transition.[15] Reliance on cause-of-death information to characterize the epidemiology of the past has led to a significant misrepresentation of the distribution of health conditions among the living. It has also promoted the view that the epidemiology of chronic diseases is more separate from that of contagious diseases than now appears to be the case.

What is the basis for the predictive capacity of Waaler surfaces and curves? Part of the answer resides in the realm of human physiology. Variations in height and weight appear to be associated with variations in the chemical composition of the tissues that make up these organs, in the quality of the electrical transmission across membranes, and in the functioning of the endocrine system and other vital systems.

Research in this area is developing rapidly, and some of the new findings have yet to be confirmed. The exact mechanisms by which malnutrition and trauma *in utero* or in early childhood are transformed into organ dysfunctions are still unclear. What is agreed upon is that the basic structure of most organs is laid down early, and it is reasonable to infer that poorly developed organs may break down earlier than well-developed ones.[16] The principal evidence so far is statistical and, despite agreement on certain specific dysfunctions, there is no generally accepted theory of cellular aging. Much of this evidence is described in Chapter 3.

Thermodynamic and Physiological Factors
in Economic Growth

So far, I have focused on the contribution of technological change to physiological improvements. However, the process has been synergistic, with improvements in nutrition and physiology contributing significantly to the process of economic growth and technological progress.

I alluded to the thermodynamic contribution to economic growth when I pointed out that individuals in the bottom 20 percent of the caloric distributions of France and England near the end of the eighteenth century lacked the energy for sustained work and were effectively excluded from the labor force. Moreover, even those who participated in the labor force had only relatively small amounts of energy for work.

Since the first law of thermodynamics applies as much to human engines as to mechanical ones, it is possible to use energy cost accounting to estimate the increase in energy available for work over the past two centuries. In the British case the thermodynamic factor explains 30 percent of the British growth rate since 1790.[17] The increase in the amount of energy available for work had two effects. It raised the labor force participation rate by bringing into the labor force the bottom 20 percent of consuming units of 1790 who had, on average, only enough energy for a few hours of slow walking. Moreover, for those in the labor force, the intensity of work per hour has increased because the number of calories available for work each day increased by about 50 percent.[18]

The physiological factor pertains to the efficiency with which the human engine converts energy input into work output. Changes in health, in the composition of diet, and in clothing and shelter can significantly affect the efficiency with which ingested energy is converted into work output. Reductions in the prevalence of infectious diseases increase the proportion of ingested energy available for work both because of savings in the energy required to mobilize the immune system and because the capacity of the gut to absorb nutrients is improved, especially as a consequence of a reduction in diarrheal diseases. Thermodynamic efficiency has also increased because of changes in the composition of the diet, including the shift from grains and other foods with high fiber content to sugar and meats. These dietary changes raised the proportion of ingested energy that can be metabolized (increased the average value of the "Atwater Factors," to use the language of nutritionists). Improvements in clothing and shelter have also increased thermodynamic efficiency by reducing the amount of energy lost through the radiation of body heat.[19]

Moreover, individuals who are stunted but otherwise healthy at maturity will be at an increased risk of incurring chronic diseases and of dying prematurely. In other words, when considered as work engines, they wear out more quickly and are less efficient at each age. The available data suggest that the average efficiency of the human engine in Britain increased by about 53 percent between 1790 and 1980. The combined effect of the increase in dietary energy available for work, and of the increased human efficiency in transforming dietary energy into work output, appears to account for about 50 percent of the British economic growth since 1790.[20]

Making Economic Sense of the Conflicts between Economic and Biomedical Measures of Inequality

As already noted, traditional economic measures of the standard of living, such as per capita income and indexes of real wages, sometimes conflict with biomedical measures such as stature, BMI, and life expectancy. What are we to make of a situation in which real wages were rising, as apparently occurred in England during the last three quarters of the nineteenth century, while working-class heights and BMI remained at relatively low levels, showing little increase over half a century? How should we characterize conditions of workers in the United States between 1820 and 1860 if real wages were generally constant or rising, sometimes quite rapidly, but heights and life expectancy were decreasing?[21] During an era in which 50 to 75 percent of the income of workers was spent on food, is it plausible that the overall standard of living of workers was improving if their nutritional status and life expectancy were declining? Although these questions are not yet resolved, they are now being vigorously investigated.[22] It may be fruitful to consider some of the new issues about the course of the standard of living and their implications for the measurement of inequality that are suggested by the anthropometric and demographic data.

If cholera and other diseases that afflicted the United States during the nineteenth century were acts of God, unrelated to the functioning of the economic system, they would pose no special problem for the resolution of the standard-of-living controversy. However, economic growth, the spread of disease, and the concomitant increase in morbidity and mortality rates were intricately intertwined. Not only was internal migration responsible for as much as 50 percent of the increase in measured per capita income during the antebellum era,[23] it was also a principal factor in the spread of cholera, typhoid, typhus, malaria, dysentery, and other major killer diseases of the era.[24] Increasing population density, another concomitant of economic growth, also increased the prevalence of various diseases, raising the level of malaria, enteric diseases, and diseases of the respiratory system.[25]

The increase in mortality between 1790 and 1860, therefore, indicates that a downward adjustment is necessary even if wage rates in high-disease localities fully reflected the extra wage compensation (which economists refer to as a "bribe") that workers demanded for the increased risks of living in these areas, since national income accounting procedures treat the bribe as an increase in national income when it is merely a cost of production. Different ways of correcting estimates of the unmeasured cost of mortality, and of adjusting the national income accounts accordingly, are discussed in the notes. They show that much of what appears to have been a rise in real wages between 1790 and 1860 is spurious, and that the apparent growth in average real wages over these years needs to be reduced by at least 40 percent.[26]

So far, I have stressed that measures of per capita income exaggerate economic growth because they fail to remove costs of production from the measure of real income. This point is akin to Simon Kuznets's correction of national income for wages paid to police because crime is not a benefit but a cost of urban production.[27] However, even when average real wages are appropriately adjusted, the bearing of this line of argument on the measurement of trends in inequality during the nineteenth century is obscure because we lack the detail needed to correct the variations of income among wage earners as well as between wage income and other types of income. The veil is lifted somewhat, however, if we switch from the conventional economic measures of inequality to the biomedical measures. Data on life expectancy in Great Britain reveal that although the life expectancy of the lower classes remained constant or declined in some localities during much of the nineteenth century, the life expectancy of the upper classes rose quite sharply. From the beginning of the Industrial Revolution to the end of the nineteenth century, the gap in life expectancy between the upper and lower classes increased by about 10 years. Similarly, the gap in stature between the upper and lower classes appears to have increased between the end of the Napoleonic wars and the beginning of the twentieth century.[28]

In other words, the biomedical data suggest that the disparity between the upper and lower classes increased during much if not most of the nineteenth century. This is a different finding than calculations based on income distributions, which suggest that during most of the nineteenth century the inequality of the English income distribution remained constant. After considering the discrepancies between the traditional economic measures and the biomedical measures, I lean toward the conclusion that for the nineteenth century the biomedical measures are more laden with economic information than the traditional economic measures, at least where assessing secular trends in inequality is concerned.[29]

A preference for biomedical measures over conventional economic measures of inequality seems even more warranted when interpreting trends in the twentieth century. In both the British and the U.S. cases, life expectancy increased dramatically between 1890 and 1930, by about 14 years in Britain (a 31 percent increase) and by about 16 years (a 36 percent increase) in the United States.[30] Over the same period, U.S. stature increased by about 6 cm. However, in both the British and American cases, measures such as the share of income held by the top 5 or 10 percent of the income distribution show that inequality was relatively constant over this period or that it might have increased slightly.[31] The experience of the Depression Decade is even more paradoxical. In the United States the unemployment rate between 1931 and 1939 varied but was never less than 16 percent; for half of the period, unemployment ranged between 20 and 25 percent. Yet life expectancy between 1929 and 1939 increased by 4 years and the heights of men reaching maturity during this period increased by 1.6 cm.[32]

The resolution of the paradox turns on the huge social investments made between 1870 and the end of World War I, whose payoffs were not counted as part of national income during the 1920s and 1930s even though they produced a large stream of benefits during these decades and continue to do so down to the present. I refer, of course, to the social investment in public health and in biomedical technology, whose largest payoffs came well after the investment was made. Included in this category are not only the direct federal investments in biomedical research, which remained modest before 1950, but also the expansion of clinical medicine practiced in a vastly expanded network of hospitals established on scientific principles, the quadrupling of higher education in medicine and the increase in the quality of that education, and the international expansion of the stock of knowledge of the biology, chemistry, and epidemiology of disease. Also included in this category are such public health investments as the construction of facilities to improve the supply of water, the purification of the milk supply, the development of effective systems of quarantines, and the cleaning of the slums.

The point is not merely that these benefits are often excluded entirely from national income accounts, and from the measures of real wages, but that they are greatly undervalued even when some aspects are included, because they are measured by inputs rather than by benefits (which are outputs). Moreover, these benefits accrued disproportionately to those with modest incomes. That those who occupy the lower rungs of society have gained more from certain forms of unmeasured income is visible in the biomedical measures because they show by how much the gap in life expectancy, in stature, and in BMI that once existed between the upper and lower income classes has been reduced.[33]

The discussion of omitted variables so far indicates that much less progress was made by the lower classes during the nineteenth century than is shown by conventional measures and that, as some have argued, the relative condition of the working class may have deteriorated during major parts of the century. The implication for the twentieth century is the reverse: omitted variables lead to an underestimate of the absolute and relative gains of the lower classes. Would these conclusions still hold if another omitted variable, leisure, was brought into consideration?

Although there were some gains in leisure for the lower class in the United States and Britain during the nineteenth century, they do not appear to have occurred until well past the middle of the century. Of the roughly 25-hour reduction in the work week between 1860 and 1990, perhaps 5 or 6 hours were eliminated before 1890. Moreover, the scope of leisure-time activities was narrow, limited primarily to frequenting bars and attending church. Drama, opera, ballet, concerts, literature, and visual arts were usually too expensive to be readily accessible to the poor. Although there were antecedents during the nineteenth century, public libraries, movies, radio, television, and the like are mainly products of the twentieth century.[34]

Kuznets, who was the leading designer of the U.S. national income accounts, recognized the large underestimate of economic growth occasioned by the omission of leisure from these accounts. Valuing the increased daily hours of leisure of workers at the average wage, he pointed out, would raise per capita income in the late 1940s by about 40 percent. Today, the figure would be closer to 120 percent. If such a computation was undertaken for each decile of the income distribution, it would be apparent that those in the top decile experienced much less of a gain in leisure, since the highly paid professionals and businessmen who populate the top decile work closer to the nineteenth-century standard of 3,200 hours per year than to the current middle-income standard of about 1,800 hours. Improvements in the variety and quality of leisure-time activities have also been less for the upper than the lower classes. The upper classes still have a proclivity for those expensive amusements that are most fully measured – opera, concerts, drama, literature. That proclivity, combined with their longer work week, means that they spend far less of their time in those forms of leisure activity for which the unmeasured gains have been greatest.[35]

The Remarkable Reduction in Inequality during the Twentieth Century

The twentieth century contrasts sharply with the record of the two preceding centuries. In every measure that we have bearing on the standard of living, such as real income, homelessness, life expectancy, and height, the gains of the lower classes have been far greater than those experienced by the population as a whole, whose overall standard of living has also improved.

The "Gini ratio," which is also called the "concentration ratio," is the measure of the inequality of the income distribution most widely used by economists.[36] This measure varies between 0 (perfect equality) and 1 (maximum inequality). In the case of England, for example, which has the longest series of income distributions, the Gini ratio stood at about 0.65 near the beginning of the eighteenth century, at about 0.55 near the beginning of the twentieth century, and at 0.32 in 1973, when it bottomed out, not only in Britain but also in the United States and other rich nations.[37] This measure indicates that over two-thirds of the reduction in the inequality of income distributions between 1700 and 1973 took place during the twentieth century. The large decrease in such inequality, coupled with the rapid increase in the average real income of the English population, means that the per capita income of the lower classes was rising much more rapidly than those of the middle or upper classes.[38]

A similar conclusion is implied by the data on life expectancies. For the cohort born about 1875, there was a gap of 17 years between the average length of life of the British elite and of the population as a whole. There is still a social gap in life expectancies among the British, but today the advantage of the richest classes over the rest of the population is only about 4 years. Thus about three-quarters of the social gap in longevity has disappeared. As a consequence, the life expectancy of the lower classes increased from 41 years at birth in 1875 to about 74 years today, while the life expectancy of the elite increased from 58 years at birth to about 78 years. That is a remarkable improvement. Indeed, there was more than twice as much increase in life expectancies during the past century as there was during the previous 200,000 years. If anything sets the twentieth century apart from the past, it is this huge increase in the longevity of the lower classes.[39]

Data on stature also indicate the high degree of inequality during the nineteenth century. At the close of the Napoleonic wars, a typical British male worker at maturity was about 5 inches shorter than a mature male of upper-class birth. There is still a gap in stature between the workers and the elite of Britain, but now the gap is only on the order of 1 inch. Height differentials by social class have virtually disappeared in Sweden and Norway but not yet in the United States. Statistical analysis across a wide array of rich and poor countries today shows a strong correlation between stature and the Gini ratio.[40]

Weight is another important measure of inequality. Despite the great emphasis in recent years on weight reduction, the world still suffers more from undernutrition and underweight than from overweight, as the World Health Organization has repeatedly pointed out. Although one should not minimize the afflictions caused by overnutrition, it is important to recognize that even in rich countries such as the United States, undernutrition remains a significant problem, especially among impoverished pregnant women, children, and the aged.

The secular increase in body builds is due primarily to the great improvement in socioeconomic conditions over the past several centuries, rather than to genetic factors, as can be seen by considering Holland. The average height of young adult males was only 64 inches in that country during the middle of the nineteenth century. The corresponding figure today is about 72 inches. An increase of 8 inches in just four generations cannot be due to natural selection or genetic drift because such processes require much longer time spans. Nor can it be attributed to heterosis (hybrid vigor) because Holland's population has remained relatively homogeneous and because the effects of heterosis in human populations have been shown both empirically and theoretically to have been quite small. It is hard to come up with credible explanations for the rapid increase in heights that do not turn on environmental factors, especially improvements in nutrition and health. These environmental factors appear to be still at work. Stature is still increasing, although at a somewhat slower rate, and nations have not yet reached a mean height that represents the biological limit of humankind under current biomedical technology.[41]

Homelessness is another indicator of the dramatic reduction in inequality during the twentieth century. Down to the middle of the nineteenth century, between 10 and 20 percent of the population in Britain and on the Continent were homeless persons whom officials classified as vagrants and paupers. Estimates of vagrancy and pauper rates in the United States during the nineteenth century are less certain, but these rates appear to have reached European levels in the major cities during the middle decades of that century. When we speak of homelessness in the United States today, we are talking about rates below 0.4 percent of the population. Many of the homeless today are mentally ill individuals prematurely released from psychiatric institutions that are inadequately funded. Many others are chronically poor and inadequately trained for the current job market.[42]

The relatively generous poverty program developed in Britain during the second half of the eighteenth century, and the bitter attacks on that program by Malthus and others, have given the unwarranted impression that government transfers played a major role in the secular decline in beggary and homelessness. Despite the relative generosity of English poor relief between 1750 and 1834, beggary and homelessness fluctuated between 10 and 20 percent. Despite the substantial reduction in the proportion of national income transferred to the poor as a result of the poor laws of 1834 and later years, homelessness declined sharply during the late nineteenth and early twentieth centuries.

The fact is that government transfers were incapable of solving the problems of beggary and homelessness during the eighteenth and much of the nineteenth centuries, because the root cause of the problems was chronic malnutrition. Even during the most generous phases of the relief program, the bottom fifth of the English population was so severely malnourished that it lacked the energy for adequate levels of work.[43]

At the end of the eighteenth century British agriculture, even when supplemented by imports, was simply not productive enough to provide more than 80 percent of the potential labor force with enough calories to sustain regular manual labor. It was the huge increases in English productivity during the later part of the nineteenth and the early twentieth centuries that made it possible to feed even the poor at relatively high caloric levels. Begging and homelessness were reduced to exceedingly low levels, by nineteenth-century standards, only when the bottom fifth of the population acquired enough calories to permit regular work. The principal way in which government policy contributed to that achievement was through its public health programs. By reducing exposure to disease, more of the calories that the poor ingested were made available for work.

3

Tragedies and Miracles in the Third World

The debate over the extent of chronic malnutrition in developing countries, which began after World War II, has been conducted largely between investigators associated with the Food and Agriculture Organization (FAO), the World Health Organization (WHO), and the World Bank, on the one hand, and critics who believe that their estimates of the extent of malnutrition are too high. I will use the acronym FAWOB to designate the investigators associated with these three organizations.

Few investigators have suggested that the FAWOB estimates are too low. One reason for the neglect of this possibility is the tendency of investigators to assume explicitly or implicitly that affluent persons in affluent countries reached their genetic potential during the middle decades of the twentieth century and that no further improvements in physiology were possible without some major genetic breakthrough. In Chapter 2, I outlined a theory of technophysio evolution that disputes that assumption. Next, I want to apply the theory of technophysio evolution to a number of problems related to health and mortality in the Third World.

Changing Views of Chronic Malnutrition and of the Methods of Measuring It

Nutritional science was still in its infancy during the early twentieth century. It was not until the turn of the century that Wilbur O. Atwater and his collaborators estimated the energy requirements of basal metabolism. Except for scurvy, specific nutrient deficiencies were not discovered until after World War I: vitamin D for rickets in 1922, thiamine for beriberi in 1933, and niacin for pellagra in 1937.[1]

By the end of World War II, nutritional science had matured to the point that it was possible to ask and provide reasonable answers to the question of the extent of malnutrition in various countries around the world. That task was undertaken by the FAO of the United Nations, which monitored the food supply through a series of surveys, the sixth of which was completed in 1996. These surveys were based on the construction of national food balance sheets that made it possible to estimate in many countries the daily number of calories available for consumption per capita. This information was supplemented by household dietary surveys based on reports of the food consumed by all the individuals in the household over periods ranging from one to several days. The food diaries generally revealed a substantially lower level of caloric consumption than did the national balance sheets. The validity of these methods of estimating the consumption of food became a central point of controversy.

Estimates of average caloric consumption per capita have been derived from three principal types of evidence: documentary sources, such as institutional food allowances or entitlements from wills; individual or household consumption surveys; and national food balance sheets. There are disadvantages to each. Records of institutional food allotments or food entitlements frequently do not indicate the age and sex of the recipients. The accuracy of individual food diaries and household consumption surveys depends on the quality of memory (and candor) of those surveyed. National food balance sheets estimate the national supply of food by subtracting allowances for seed and feed, losses in processing, changes in inventories, and net exports (positive or negative) from the national annual production of each crop, thereby obtaining a residual of grains and vegetables available for consumption. When using national food balance sheets, not only must the calories be calculated accurately, but losses due to poor storage, food processing, and individual waste must also be factored into the estimate of calories consumed. Recent metabolic studies have shown that national food balance sheets provide a more accurate measure of average caloric intake than food diaries.[2]

Equally controversial were efforts to estimate average physiological requirements of energy in countries around the world.[3] In addition to estimating the energy required for basal metabolism, it was necessary to estimate the minimal amount of energy required for maintenance as well as the specific amounts of energy required for different tasks. The work of numerous investigators on these issues was summarized and synthesized in a series of expert consultations. Published in 1953, 1973, and 1985, these consultations yielded somewhat contradictory assessments of all three categories of energy requirement: basal metabolism, maintenance, and activities.[4]

An important shift in the conception of nutritional diseases began in the late 1950s and extended through the mid-1970s. Prior to that period, nutritional diseases were limited to those caused by specific nutrient deficiencies, such as pellagra, rickets, and beriberi. General undernutrition, so widespread in developing nations, was considered to be a normal, if undesirable, characteristic of these societies. During the 1950s and 1960s, physicians, nutritionists, and epidemiologists began to define substantial undernutrition as a disease called "protein-energy malnutrition" (PEM).[5] In the *Ninth International Classification of Diseases* and in WHO publications, anthropometric indicators are used to specify the degree of PEM. However, the early developers of the concept of PEM focused not on adult heights and weights, but on the heights and weights of children under 5. For such children they emphasized such measures as low weight-for-age, low weight-for-height, and low height-for-age.

Low weight-for-height or weight-for-age is called "wasting" and low height-for-age is called "stunting." A series of studies during the 1970s and 1980s demonstrated that weight at given ages, weight-for-height, and height-for-age were effective predictors of the risk of morbidity and mortality among children under 5.[6]

Perhaps the most important development during this period was the discovery of a synergy between infections and malnutrition. Scrimshaw, Taylor, and Gordon (1968) showed that while malnutrition makes infections more severe, infections in turn increase the severity of malnutrition. Mechanisms through which malnutrition reduces resistance to infection include reduced production of humoral antibodies (protective substances in blood or tissue fluid), impaired cell-mediated immunity (immunity mediated by active cells such as white blood cells), and weakened phagocytosis (the engulfment and digestion of bacteria and other foreign particles by a cell). Conversely, infections, regardless of the nature of the infectious agent, worsen nutritional status through increased metabolic loss of nutrients, reduced appetite, decreased absorption, and the diversion of nutrients to combat the infection.

The transformation of undernutrition from a normal condition to a disease intensified the criticisms of the FAWOB approach to chronic malnutrition. Three main lines of criticism emerged. It was argued, first, that methods of constructing food balance sheets grossly exaggerated the level of nutrient consumption in rich countries (by underestimating losses in distribution and plate waste) and underestimated the nutrients available in poor countries (by omitting nonstandard types of foods). Second, the threshold of malnutrition was overestimated by a failure to take adequate account of the extent to which undernourished individuals could successfully adapt to their situation.[7] The third line of criticism focused on the use of the U.S. and British growth standards as a basis for judging stunting and wasting among individuals in South Asia and other regions in which malnutrition was prevalent. The counter-interpretation was summed up by the aphorism "small but healthy."[8]

The Implications of Technophysio Evolution for the Assessment of Chronic Malnutrition

A difficulty with the FAWOB approach to the measurement of chronic malnutrition is that their standards are based on heights and weights derived either from British body builds of the early 1960s and 1970s or from U.S. body builds of the early 1970s. Neither the British nor the Americans claim that their body builds are optimal. They claim only that they are representative of the actual distribution of height, weight, and weight-for-height at specific ages in their respective countries. In practice, however, it has been assumed that the 50th centile of these distributions is optimal.

Should the 50th centile of the British and American height distributions be accepted as the standard for developing nations? Critics of FAWOB have called these standards too high. However, a study of growth patterns of Indian children revealed that the age-specific height and weight distributions of affluent Indian children were quite similar to the distributions at corresponding ages obtained from the United States and Great Britain.[9]

That finding, important as it is, does not settle the issue. It merely confirms that the environmental constraints on the growth of affluent Indians are similar to those prevailing in Britain. The finding does not demonstrate that affluent Indian children are not stunted relative to their genetic potential, nor does it establish that the 50th centile of the British and American height distributions is optimal.

The Problem of Perspective in an Age of Technophysio Evolution

If human physiology were static, there would be far less difficulty in establishing anthropometric standards for measuring chronic malnutrition in poor nations. However, as is illustrated by Figure 3.1, there have been enormous changes in British physiology over the past two centuries.[10] That figure presents the bottom half of the current Dutch growth chart. This is the kind of chart that pediatricians use to assess whether a child of a given age is developing

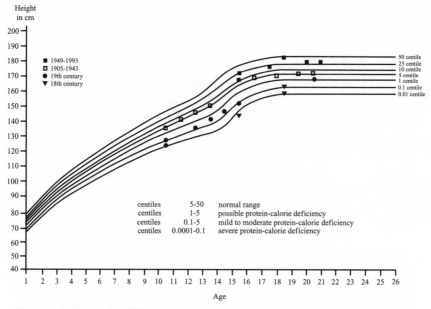

Figure 3.1 Secular Trends in the Average Heights of Male Adolescents in Great Britain, 1748–1993, Relative to Current Dutch Growth Curves.

Source: I am indebted to Roderick Floud for these data.

normally. The average heights of successive generations of male adolescents in Great Britain between 1748 and 1993 are superimposed on that grid. It can be seen that as one generation succeeded another, the average trajectory of adolescent growth moved up the grid, although the upward movement was uneven. The largest increase took place during the twentieth century.

Obviously, a judgment of the severity of malnutrition in India today depends on which of the height profiles shown in Figure 3.1 is chosen as the standard. Suppose that we used not the British height profiles of the 1960s as the standard for judging the deficit in current Indian stature, but those of the 1920s, which were only at the 5th centile of the current Dutch standard (see Figure 3.1). The switch to the British standard of the 1920s would make Indian malnutrition today seem less severe because the nutritional status of

British children 70 years ago was relatively poor by current Dutch standards. Even British children of the early 1960s fall substantially short of the current Dutch standard.[11]

I have used the Dutch standard to assess British stature because the Dutch are currently the tallest population in the world, with males averaging about 181 cm at maturity, which is about 4 cm greater than the stature of mature males in both Britain and the United States today. In 1860, however, Dutch males were only 164 cm at maturity. British and American males were also shorter at maturity in 1860 than they are today, but in 1860 the British were 4 cm taller than the Dutch, while the Americans were 8 cm taller than the Dutch. In other words, heights have grown substantially over the past four generations in all three societies. But the Dutch have grown most rapidly, partly because they were more stunted during the nineteenth century than were either the British or the Americans.[12]

Notice that a height of 164 cm at maturity would put the Dutch of 1860 below the first percentile of the current Dutch height distribution (see Figure 3.1). In other words, if we use the current Dutch standard, we would conclude that the Dutch in 1860 and the Indians in the 1980s suffered from similar degrees of chronic malnutrition. On the other hand, if we used the Dutch height distribution of 1860 as the standard for good nutritional status, Indians in the 1980s would be judged to have good levels of nutrition.

Obviously, it makes no sense to use European height distributions that go back to a time when Europeans were severely malnourished as a standard of good nutrition. Of course, nobody three or four generations ago realized that children who were then of average stature or weight were severely malnourished since they had no way of predicting that stature and weight would increase as much as they have. The question is, are the British and other West Europeans as well as North Americans still malnourished by standards that will prevail in the future? Can we rule out the possibility that body builds in these populations will increase as much in the next century as they did in the previous one?

Accelerating Technological Change and Diffusion

The answers to these questions turn on two issues. One issue concerns the past and the likely future of technological change. The other is the past and the likely future of technologically induced physiological change. In Chapter 2, I emphasized the enormous acceleration in the rate of technological change after 1700, especially after 1900.

Not only has productive technology changed dramatically, but the diffusion of modern technology has also accelerated greatly over the past two centuries. Modern economic growth began first in Great Britain early in the eighteenth century. It did not begin in the United States until the late eighteenth century. France joined them after the Napoleonic era. By the middle of the nineteenth century, the circle had expanded to include the Netherlands, Germany, Switzerland, Denmark, Norway, Sweden, Canada, and Australia. Japan, Russia, and Argentina did not embark on the path of modern economic growth until the end of the nineteenth century. For Italy and other West European nations, modern economic growth was delayed until the beginning of the twentieth century. Except for Japan, modern economic growth did not extend to Asia until after World War II.

Today, however, the most remarkable instances of rapid economic growth are in Asian and Latin American countries, which together represent more than half of the population of the world. Beginning in the early 1950s, first Japan, then the Asian Tigers (South Korea, Taiwan, Singapore, and Hong Kong), and more recently China, Malaysia, Thailand, Indonesia, India, and more than a dozen other countries in Eastern Europe, Asia, and Latin America, often referred to as "emerging market economies," began growing in both gross domestic product and product per capita at rates that far exceeded the long-term experience of the early leaders. Japan has set the standard for this pattern. Its gross domestic product increased by 14-fold in just four decades, transforming Japan from an impoverished land with characteristics typical of countries at low levels of development into the second wealthiest nation in the world. That large a leap took nearly a century and a half in the West. In France, for example, it stretched from 1820 to 1969; in Great Britain, from 1820 to 1967.[13]

The Interdependence of Industrial Progress and Public Health in the Long Run

The acceleration of economic growth in the high-performing Asian economies (HPAEs) is due in large measure to the rich and varied stock of technologies available to them, far greater than that available to the early leaders. Nobel laureates Simon Kuznets and Theodore W. Schultz emphasized the role played by the backlog of technologies in the rapid recovery of Europe after World War II. Kuznets also emphasized that some technological breakthroughs, such as electrical power, permitted increases in economic productivity across the spectrum of activities. However, applying that source of energy to particular uses required specific additional technological innovations, such as fractional horsepower motors to transmit electrical power to machines operating at various speeds, vacuum tubes to permit reception of radio signals, and third rails or overhead power lines to permit vehicular movement. Similarly, lines of chemical investigation pursued in one industry, such as the development of new dyes for textiles, new reactive agents for steel, new preservatives for foods, the fortification of flour, and the transformation of coal into textiles, often provided the basis for unseen applications in remote industries and contributed to the emergence of many new branches of chemistry.[14]

Urbanization and Public Health

The rapid diffusion of water purification and waste removal technologies among the cities of the Third World, as compared with their painfully slow diffusion among the European and American countries that led the Industrial Revolution, is a case in point. The initial impact of the urban growth spurt of the nineteenth century was to increase morbidity and mortality because city size outran the existing capacities of water delivery, sewage removal, and housing. The delivery of pure water and the removal of waste in cities as massive as London, Paris, and New York during the second half of the nineteenth century required major advances in hydraulic equipment, in pipes of varying materials to deliver the water and carry off the waste, and in new construction techniques required to build tunnels over long distances, to build canals and reservoirs, and to build sewage farms and destructors for the disposal of refuse. Cities such as New York hired chemists to analyze regularly the contents of the water. In his annual report for 1871, the chemist of the City of New York reported on the impurities found in the residential water supply, including lead, since many streets were laid with lead pipe. When questioned about the levels of lead, the chemist replied that the principal alternative to lead was iron pipes coated with zinc, and doubted that consuming minute quantities of lead was worse than consuming similar amounts of zinc.[15] It took more than half a century before chemists could provide correct assessments of the dangers from lead and even longer to assess the desired levels of zinc.[16]

Time and industrial experience were also needed to settle such issues as whether the dumping of wastewater and sewage back into rivers or into cesspools was really inferior to sewage treatment and filtration through sand. Efforts at assessment were confounded by perverse changes in infant and childhood deaths during the four decades preceding World War I, suggesting to many that the changes in mortality rates were unrelated to the nature of sanitary programs in different towns. As experts debated various alternatives, often ridiculing each other's theories, politicians worried about the public's tolerance for extremely expensive projects that only a small fraction of households were willing to buy on their own. In many French towns at the turn of the twentieth century, for example, fewer than 10 percent of the households subscribed to the delivery of pure water or the new methods of removing waste.[17]

Drainage of swamps was often an unplanned by-product of urban expansion or the growth of demand for agricultural products.

For example, the drainage of Ohio swamps during the last decades of the nineteenth century and the early decades of the twentieth century was due to the rising cost of farmland, which made the retrieval of swampy land a profitable enterprise. The reduced prevalence of malaria was an unexpected boon, much to be desired although hardly something that a land developer could expect to profit from, even if he actually connected the benefit to his enterprise. Similarly, the considerable expansion of acreage devoted to beet sugar or tobacco, and the increased investment in the production of beef, pork, and (later) chicken, were responses to market forces rather than the implementation of programs to improve health.[18]

The West served as an experimental laboratory from which the countries of the Third World could learn when they entered their phase of rapid urbanization. Consequently, rather than acting as a barrier to improvements in health and longevity, as it had in Europe and America during the nineteenth century, the rapid expansion of cities in the Third World after World War II served to increase longevity in the respective countries.[19]

Technological Progress in Food Production

The massive food shortages created by World War II exacerbated the pressures on food supplies due to the continuing worldwide decline in mortality rates and the concomitant acceleration of population growth. The new mortality declines of the 1950s and 1960s were most rapid in Asia, promoted in part by the massive postwar programs of malaria eradication and food supplementation. The enormous acceleration of population growth in countries such as India and Ceylon, coupled with the disorganization of native agricultural production sometimes associated with food aid, created alarms about impending disaster. Theories that population growth made Malthusian-type famines imminent gained support from the Great Bengal Famine of the 1940s, which was initially ascribed to bad crops. Not until the 1980s did it become known that the Bengal famine and other food disasters were actually due to breakdowns in the system of food distribution, often brought on by perverse government policies, rather than actual shortages of food.[20]

In fact, despite the postwar doubling of the Asian population in just a few decades, advances in seeds, dry farming techniques, improved fertilizer, new crops, and the expansion of arable land have permitted a vast increase in the world's food supply. Not only has agricultural production kept pace with the population explosion of the past half century, but the world's per capita consumption of food has actually increased, rising by about 0.6 percent per annum over the past several decades.[21]

Taking Account of Technophysio Evolution in Setting Standards for Chronic Malnutrition

The fact that the availability of dietary energy increased by about 400 calories per capita worldwide between 1965 and 1989 does not imply that the problem of chronic malnutrition in poor countries has been solved. Levels of food consumption in India are still below those that prevailed in Western Europe in the mid-nineteenth century. Whether assessed by minimally adequate levels of caloric and protein intake or by current anthropometric standards, it remains true that about 15 percent of the world's population suffers from chronic malnutrition.[22]

Indeed, arguments used to condemn FAWOB standards as exaggerated that seemed compelling in the early 1980s have been shown to be unwarranted. It is not true that dietary interviews are more reliable than national food balance sheets in estimating average caloric consumption. New procedures, such as the doubly labeled water method, which measure the energy actually metabolized, have shown that dietary surveys actually underestimate caloric consumption by about 25 percent. Thus national food balance sheets are a better measure of average caloric consumption, especially for the estimation of long-term trends, than was previously assumed. These new procedures also undermine the contention of statistician P. V. Sukhatme and others that the boundary of chronic malnutrition should be increased by several hundred calories on the ground that the variance of the caloric distribution has been underestimated because of the neglect of *intra*individual variance (the day-to-day variation in food consumption that is normal in individual diets).[23] Metabolic analysis has shown that the variance of the food distribution is due overwhelmingly to *inter*individual variations in food intake and activity levels. Moreover, when energy intake and physical activity are controlled, *intra*individual variance is insignificant.

The Failure to Take Account of Technophysio Evolution

In fact, FAWOB has underestimated the extent of chronic malnutrition because of a failure to take account of technophysio evolution. As I indicated earlier, a number of recent studies suggest that current mean body builds, even in countries abundant in calories, still appear to be suboptimal when the optimal height and BMI are defined as those that minimize the age-specific odds of dying or of developing chronic diseases over a specific interval. Moreover, trends in nutritional status and risk vary significantly even among rich countries. This point is illustrated by Figure 3.2.

Superimposed on the Waaler surface in Figure 3.2 are rough estimates of the average heights and weights in both France and England at several dates between 1705 and 2001. In 1705 the French were not only much shorter but their BMIs were much lower than those of the English. During the nineteenth century the French caught up with, and by 1867 exceeded, the English in BMI. However, they remained several centimeters shorter than the English. Between 1867 and 1967 French stature remained below that of the English, but the gap narrowed and the French achieved higher BMIs. Still, down to the mid-twentieth century, the English advantage in height more than offset the French advantage in BMI with respect to the risk of death. After 1967, French stature increased quite rapidly and its BMI moved closer to the optimal level, mainly because at taller heights, lower BMIs are optimal. During the same period, English gains in stature were modest, but their

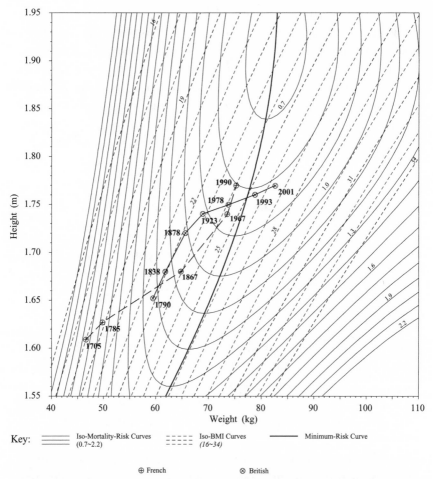

Key: ═══ Iso-Mortality-Risk Curves (0.7~2.2)   ----- Iso-BMI Curves (16~34)   ── Minimum-Risk Curve

⊕ French   ⊗ British

Figure 3.2 Waaler Surface of Relative Mortality Risk for Height and Weight among Norwegian Males Aged 50–64 with a Plot of the Estimated French and English Heights and Weights since 1705 at Ages 25–39.

Sources: French: for 1705, 1785, 1867, and 1967 see Figure 2.4. The height for the 1990 data point is from Cavelaars et al. 2000; the BMI for 1990 is assumed to be the same as the 1980 BMI in Rolland-Cachera et al. 1991. British: 1790 point is from Fogel, Floud, and Harris, n.d. Points for 1838, 1878, 1923, and 1978 are from Floud 1998, Table 6. Points for 1993 and 2001 are from the Health Survey for England (see Tables 4, 5, and 6 at http://www.doh.gov.uk/stats/trends1.htm).

Note: For a brief description of the procedure used to estimate the British point for 1780, see Fogel 1997; a more extensive explanation appears in Fogel, Floud, and Harris, n.d. This figure supersedes versions that have appeared previously.

BMI increased so rapidly that by 2001 they were well in excess of the optimal level for their height. As a consequence, by the 1990s English mortality risk associated with body builds exceeded that of the French. Although their statures were equal, the English were at a disadvantage because their BMI shot past the optimal level.

Thus Figure 3.2 illustrates how technophysio evolution conquered the severe malnutrition of past centuries. But in so doing, it created a new problem: overnutrition. Food has become so cheap that corpulence is no longer a sign of opulence. It is instead a sign of weakness of will.

Have Waaler curves and surfaces been changing over time? It is too soon to answer that question with any confidence. Work is currently underway to construct Waaler curves and surfaces from morbidity and mortality data obtained from a large sample of data from Union Army veterans covering the period between 1890 and 1930. Preliminary analysis based on a small subsample (and reported in Figure 1.2) suggests that the curve in BMI and mortality for these men is quite similar to that shown for Norwegian males.[24]

On the other hand, Figure 3.3 provides some support for the hypothesis that what is optimal with respect to body builds may be changing slowly under the impact of technophysio evolution. That figure presents the perinatal death rate by birth weight in three populations. For babies born to U.S. mothers, who had relatively large body builds, the birth weight that minimized the perinatal death rate was about 3500 grams. But for babies born to Ghanaian and Indian mothers, who had relatively small body builds, the birth weight that minimized the perinatal death rate was about 2600 grams – barely above the U.S. level of dangerously small babies.

This finding may bear on the explanation of the first phase of the secular decline in mortality. Some investigators have called attention to changes in age-specific mortality rates that may indicate a shift in the balance between pathogens and their human hosts. Although the shift has been attributed to a decline in the virulence of pathogens, not enough evidence is in hand to assess this possibility. However, the recent physiological research summarized in

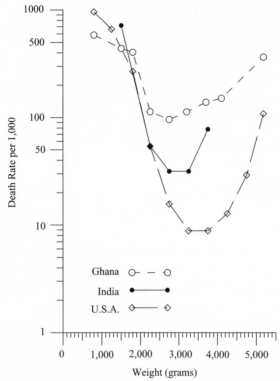

Figure 3.3 Perinatal Death Rate by Birth Weight in Ghana, India, and the United States.
Source: Hytten and Leitch 1971.

this section suggests a new pathway through which the balance between pathogens and human hosts may have turned in favor of the hosts. In addition to the improved operation of the immune system, there is the increased capacity of a vital organ to survive the attack of pathogens as a result of increased tissue resilience, including the improved operation of the nervous system. The process could have been synergistic since the improvement in the operation of the immune system might have interacted with the increased resilience of other vital organs. Such possible synergies call into question the proposition that because an individual appears to be currently well fed, malnutrition does not affect the outcome of diseases such as influenza, smallpox, or typhoid. Individuals may be more likely to succumb to such infections, even if they are currently well fed, because past malnutrition, either *in utero* or subsequently, has degraded vital organs.

Implications for the Use of NCHS or British Standards

Although U.S. and British children and adults live longer and have less disease than their counterparts in South Asia, the work on Waaler surfaces indicates that current final heights and current BMIs in the United States and Britain may be suboptimal.[25] There is, of course, the question of whether any society can reach an average height for males of 190 cm. Although no society has yet reached that average, the possibility cannot now be ruled out. Few, if any, persons alive in 1800 forecast the increases in European stature that occurred during the subsequent two centuries.[26]

Continued use of the NCHS standards for assessing the extent of malnutrition in less developed nations is feasible. But it should be understood that these standards may not indicate all the physiological improvements that are obtainable through an improvement in nutrition and in other environmental advances. Pending further evidence, an interim change worthy of consideration is making the growth curves of the Netherlands the international standard, since this is the nation that has so far achieved the greatest improvement in nutritional status.[27]

Physiological Capital and the Adaptation Controversy: Implications for the Measurement of Economic Growth

Figure 2.4 makes it clear that the limitation of body size has been one of the principal ways of adapting to low levels of energy. The point is not merely that height and BMI increased as the per capita supply of food increased. It is also that increases and decreases in body size represent changes in physiological capacity that affected both the quality of life and the capacity to produce. Consequently, when traditional agricultural technology was too inefficient to sustain a large average body size, it also limited the capacity to acquire physiological capital. Under the prevailing agricultural technology of 1800, Frenchmen could not have achieved the physiological capacity associated with modern body sizes. If Frenchmen in 1800 had been as large on average as they are today, there would not have been enough energy to produce the food supply, since all of the available energy would have been required for basal metabolism.

Viewed historically, it makes little sense to talk about whether wasting or stunting is a desirable form of adaptation since there was no alternative. Indeed, only when the technology of food production became much more efficient than it had been during the eighteenth century did it become possible to sustain large people. It was only at that point that individuals generally could have chosen between more energy and more industrial goods or other nonfood commodities.

Figures 2.4 and 2.7 imply that the cost of adaptation to inadequate food supplies paid by wasted and stunted individuals cannot be measured merely by using cross-sectional data (data generated during a given year) to determine whether productivity is positively correlated with stature. Such cross-sectional procedures do not take into account the rate of decline in human capital over the life cycle. Since stunting accelerates the rate of depreciation in human capital over the life cycle, the discounted present value of output is, on average, lower than that inferred from cross-sections.[28] Even if, at a given age, a short person who is still in the labor force is as productive as a tall one, more short than tall persons of that age have left the labor force because of disability or death.[29] Hence, there is sample selection bias in econometric studies that omit from consideration those members of a cohort who are no longer in the labor force. Even studies that show a positive effect of stature or BMI on output have biased the effect downward unless they have taken account of the omitted observations.

Figures 2.4 and 2.7 also point to another problem that is often overlooked. To equalize the rate of depreciation in physiological capital, stunted individuals require higher BMIs than tall individuals. For example, to equalize the odds of retaining good health in middle age, a person of 165 cm needs a BMI that is

25 percent higher than that of a person of 181 cm. Moreover, when risks are equalized, the BMI of the stunted individual is greater than that of the tall individual. Figures 2.4 and 2.7 imply, therefore, that adaptation to malnutrition by saving on the energy for basal metabolism requires an increased rate of depreciation in physiological capital. Hence, the essence of adaptation via body size to an inadequate food supply is a trade-off of current metabolic needs for an increased life-cycle risk of mortality. For example, a male who is 165 cm in height, and who saves on food by losing enough weight to reduce his requirement for basal metabolism by 5 percent, will increase his risk of mortality by 15 percent.

Figures 3.4 and 3.5 were constructed by John Kim to describe a hitherto neglected aspect of what economists call "health capital." In this case, the Waaler surface is interpreted as a "health-production" surface. Up to a certain point, people can produce better health by raising children with greater stature and greater BMIs. Figure 3.4 portrays the region of efficient body builds for the production of good health. This efficient zone is denoted by the two heavy black lines intersecting the iso-morbidity curves. The right-hand locus has already been introduced. It is the curve connecting the minimum points of each iso-morbidity curve, which I previously referred to as the optimum weight curve. It is the locus of all points on the iso-morbidity curves with a zero slope.

The left-hand boundary is the locus of all of the points on the health isoquants in which the slopes turn from negative to positive. According to the economic theory of production, efficient production takes place only in regions where isoquants have negative slopes. Kim uses this theory to predict that the production level of good health will not normally take place on an isoquant with a positive slope, because it is possible to produce a given level of health with a smaller amount of nutritional resources by moving down the isoquant – toward the point at which the tangent to the isoquant is vertical.

In Figure 3.5 Kim shows that his prediction does indeed hold for data aggregated at the national level. It shows the points indicating the mean heights and weights of adult males in 140 countries in

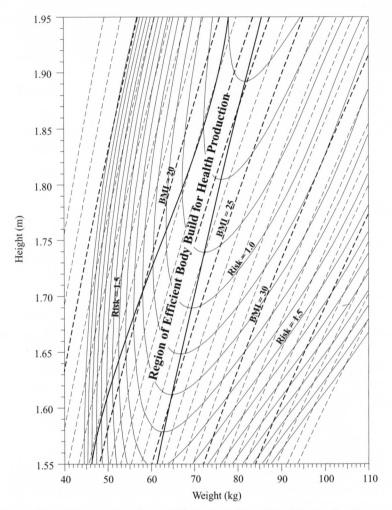

Figure 3.4 Efficient Region of Body Build for Health Production on a Waaler Surface in Mortality for Norwegian Males Aged 45–89.
Source: Reprinted from Kim 1996, p. 89, with the permission of the author.

1990. All but a handful of these countries are located within the efficient zone. Just five rich nations in Europe and North America are located to the right of the efficient zone, and three poor nations in Asia and Africa are located to the left of the efficient zone. It is also worth noting that Figure 3.5 provides cross-sectional evidence

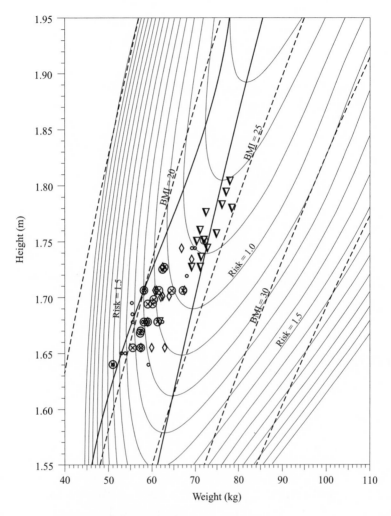

Key: ⊗: Africa & Middle East
     ▽: Europe & North America
     ○: Asia & Oceania
     ◊: Central and South America

Figure 3.5 Mean Height and Weight of 140 Adult Male Populations in 1990.

Source: Reprinted from Kim 1996, p. 90, with the permission of the author.

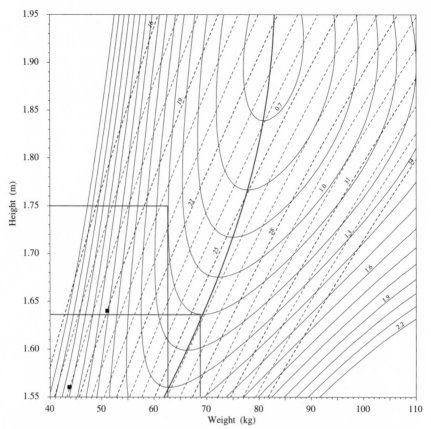

Figure 3.6 Iso-Mortality Curves of Relative Risk for Height and Weight among Norwegian Males Aged 50–64, with Two Plots. The small, dark squares show the effect of a 5 percent reduction in height and weight on the risk of dying. The large rectangles show the increase in weight required to offset the increased risk of dying due to long-term reductions in stature.

of the association between physiological capital and economic growth, since poor countries of Africa and the Middle East are located in the southwest quadrant, while the rich countries of Europe and North America fall in the northeast quadrant.

Figure 3.6 calls attention to another problem that is often overlooked. To equalize the rate of depreciation in human capital, stunted individuals require higher BMIs than tall individuals. Earlier, it was noted that to equalize the odds of retaining good health in middle age, a male of 165 cm needs a BMI that is substantially higher than that of a male of 181 cm. However, when risks are equalized (i.e., when two or more sets of height and weight points lie on the same iso-mortality curve), the BMR of the stunted individual is higher than that of the tall individual. Figure 3.6 demonstrates that saving on the energy for basal metabolism requires an increased rate of depreciation in human capital. Hence, the essence of adaptation via body size to an inadequate food supply is a trade-off of current metabolic needs for an increased life-cycle risk of morbidity and mortality.[30] Indeed, in the case illustrated in Figure 3.6, a long-run (over several decades) adaptation to a reduction in the food supply through a 5 percent reduction in stature and BMI requires a 19 percent increase in the risk of dying. In the short run, adaptation can only occur in weight (height remaining constant). The necessary weight reduction would be about 14 percent and the risk of mortality would rise by 35 percent. Hence, short-run adaptations are riskier than those that occur in the long run because of the distortion in body proportions.[31]

As a Chicago economist, I cannot resist pointing out that in adaptation through stunting or wasting, as in so many other circumstances, there is no such thing as a free lunch.

4

Prospects for the Twenty-First Century

A specter is haunting the OECD nations. It is not the specter of poverty or class warfare, as was the case a century ago, when leisure was the privilege of the very rich and workers toiled from sunrise to sunset to earn enough to purchase meager amounts of food, clothing, and shelter. In 1890, retirement was a rare phenomenon. Virtually all workers died while still in the labor force. Today, half of those in the labor force, supported by generous pensions, retire in their fifties.

To many of today's political leaders this situation, the realization of the dreams of reformers a century ago, is a potential disaster. With the baby-boom generation of 1945–65 now approaching retirement, they are confronted with the choice between defaulting on commitments to retirees, delaying the age of retirement, or increasing the taxes borne by young workers. The specter that now haunts OECD nations is not class warfare but intergenerational warfare.

The Impact of Technophysio Evolution on Work and Consumption

How did this crisis arise? The brief answer is *technophysio evolution*. Over the past century, technophysio evolution has permitted the average length of retirement to increase by five-fold, the proportion of a cohort that lives to retire to increase by seven-fold, and the amount of leisure time available to those still in the labor force to increase by nearly four-fold.

Since technophysio evolution is still ongoing, it is likely that improvements in health, life expectancy, and average income will also continue. One concomitant of these changes has been a change in the structure of consumption. A century ago, the typical household in OECD nations spent over 80 percent of its income on food, clothing, and shelter. Today these commodities account for less than a third of consumption. Many people are alarmed at this and other recent changes in the structure of consumption, particularly the reduced role of manufacturing, which they fear may presage economic and social decadence and portend a reversal in national fortunes, not only because of romantic attachment to the rust-belt industries but also because of the reduced employment in these industries.[1] A similar state of mind was widespread at the end of the nineteenth century. But then it was the decline of agriculture and the rise of industry that was the focus of concern. Those who identified the good life with agriculture were fearful of life in an urban and industrial age. Now it is life in a service society that promotes anxiety.[2]

Changes in Hours of Work and Use of Time

Of the 24 hours in a day, only 14 hours are discretionary, since 10 hours a day are biologically determined by requirements of sleep, eating, and vital hygiene. The changing ways in which individuals make use of their discretionary time have recently emerged as a political issue. The decline in hours of work, the rise in unemployment, and the threatened "end of the job" also create anxiety,

Table 4.1 Secular Trends in Time Use: The Average Hourly Division of the Day of the Average Male Household Head (based on a 365-day work year)

	c. 1880	c. 1995	c. 2040
1. Sleep	8	8	8
2. Meals and essential hygiene	2	2	2
3. Chores[a]	2	2	2
4. Travel to and from work[b]	1	1	0.5
5. Work[c]	8.5	4.7	3.8
6. Illness[d]	0.7	0.5	0.5
7. Subtotal	22.2	18.2	16.8
8. Residual for leisure activities[e]	1.8	5.8	7.2

[a] Includes chopping firewood, shoveling coal, repairs in homes, of fences, and so on, maintaining tools, gardening, carting, weaving and sewing, and care of children and the aged. Much of what was called "chores" is now called "do-it-yourself" and "sweat equity."

[b] In the case of farm laborers, travel is the walk from cottages to fields where work was conducted.

[c] In c. 1880: calculated on 3,109 annual hours. It assumes a 64-hour work week, 7 days of holidays, and 18 days of illness. In 1995: calculated on 1,730 annual hours. It assumes a 37.5-hour work week, 28 holidays, and 14 sick days. In 2040: calculated on 1,400 annual hours. It assumes a 30-hour work week, 30 holidays, and 12 sick days.

[d] Sick days in c. 1880 and c. 1995 are based on U.S. data and are applied to the 14 discretionary hours.

[e] Includes travel time to and from leisure-time activities. In c. 1880, seven holidays at 14 hours per day discretionary time provide 0.3 hour of leisure per day on a 365-day basis. The corresponding figures are 1.1 hours per day in 1995 and 1.2 hours per day in 2040.

Source: Fogel 2000.

although there is another way of looking at these phenomena.[3] Table 4.1, line 5, shows the remarkable reduction in average daily work that has occurred for males in the U.S. labor force over the past century.[4] It also forecasts the future division of the average day, indicating that by 2040 more than half of the discretionary day will be devoted to leisure activities. The forecast is for a reduction of the work year from the current average of about 1,730 hours to just 1,400 hours (it was 3,100 hours in 1880), with the average work week down to 30 hours, paid holidays up to 30, and sick days at 14.

The work day of women in 1880 was somewhat longer, and in some respects may have been more arduous, than that of men. There is evidence suggesting that the female work day in 1880 may have run about 15 minutes longer than that of males, amounting to perhaps 8.75 hours per day, on the basis of a 365-day year, or about 3,200 hours annually.[5]

As a result of the mechanization of the household, smaller families per household, and the marketing of prepared foods, the typical nonemployed married woman today spends about 3.4 hours per day engaged in housework; and if she is employed, the figure drops to 2.1 hours. However, women in the labor force average about 4.6 hours per day as employees. Hence combining "work" with "chores," men and women work roughly equal amounts per day, and both enjoy much more leisure than they used to. The principal difference is that the gains of women have come exclusively from the reduction in hours of housework, while the gains of men have come from the reduction in the hours of employed work.[6]

I have so far retained the common distinction between "work" and "leisure," although these terms are already inaccurate and may soon be obsolete. This distinction was invented when most people were engaged in manual labor for 60 or 70 hours per week and was intended to contrast with the elevated activities of the gentry or their American equivalent, Thorstein Veblen's "leisure class."[7] However, it should not be assumed that members of the leisure class were indolent. In their youth they were students and athletes. In their young adult years they were warriors. In their middle and later ages they were judges, ministers of state, parliamentarians, bishops, landlords, planters, merchant princes, other high officeholders, and patrons of the arts. Whatever they did was for the pleasure it gave them since they were so rich that earning money was not their concern.

Hence, leisure is not a synonym for indolence but a reference to desirable forms of effort or work ("work" is to be understood here in the physiological rather than the economic sense). As George Bernard Shaw put it, "labor is doing what we must; leisure is doing what we like; and rest is doing nothing whilst our bodies and our minds are recovering from their fatigue."[8] To some extent presently, and more so in the future as the average work week declines toward 28 hours and retirement normally begins at age 55, these terms will lose their pejorative connotation. Work will increasingly mean activity under the compulsion of earning income, regardless of whether the effort is manual or mental. And leisure will mean purely voluntary activity, as was characteristic of the English gentry or Veblen's American leisure class, although it may incidentally produce income. In order to avoid confusion, I reserve the word "work" for use in its physiological sense, an activity that requires energy above BMR and maintenance. Activity aimed primarily at earning a living I will call "earnwork." Purely voluntary activity, even if it incidentally carries some payment with it, I will call "volwork."

It is not only daily and weekly hours of earnwork that have declined. The share of lifetime discretionary hours spent in earnwork has declined even more rapidly. Table 4.1 does not reflect the fact that the average age on entering the labor force is about 5 years later today than it was in 1880, that the number of holidays during the work year has substantially increased, or that the expected average period of retirement for those who live to age 20 is about 11 years longer today than it was in 1880.[9]

Thus, contrary to much of public opinion, the lifetime discretionary hours spent earning a living have declined by about one-third over the past century (see Table 4.2) despite the large increase in the total of lifetime discretionary time. In 1880 four-fifths of discretionary time was spent earning a living. Today, the lion's share (59 percent) is spent doing what we like. Moreover, it appears probable that by 2040, close to 75 percent of discretionary time will be spent doing what we like, despite a further substantial increase in discretionary time due to the continuing extension of the life span.

Why do so many people want to forgo earnwork that would allow them to buy more food, clothing, housing, and other goods? The answer turns partly on the extraordinary technological change of the past century, which has not only greatly reduced the number of hours of labor the average individual needs to obtain his or her

Table 4.2 Estimated Trend in the Lifetime Distribution
of Discretionary Time

	1880	1995	2040
1. Lifetime discretionary hours	225,900	298,500	321,900
2. Lifetime earnwork hours	182,100	122,400	75,900
3. Lifetime volwork hours	43,800	176,100	246,000

Note: Discretionary time excludes time required for sleep, eating, and vital hygiene, which is taken to require an average of 10 hours per day. The availability of discretionary time is taken to commence with the average age of entry into the labor force and includes chores, travel to and from earnwork, and earnwork. Expected years of life after entering the labor force is 41.9 in 1880, 53.0 in 1995, and 62 in 2040. Expected years in the labor force at time of entry is 40.1 in 1880, 40.3 years in 1995, and 33 years in 2040.
Source: Fogel 2000.

food supply, but has also made housing, clothing, and a vast array of consumer durables so cheap in real terms that total material consumption requires far fewer hours of labor today than was required over a lifetime for food alone in 1880.

Indeed, we have become so rich that we are approaching saturation in the consumption not only of necessities, but also of goods recently thought to be luxuries or that existed only as dreams of the future during the first third of the twentieth century. Today there is an average of nearly two cars per household in the United States. Virtually everyone who is old enough and well enough to drive a car has one. In the case of television, there are 0.8 sets per person (2.2 per household). In some items such as radios, we seem to have reached supersaturation, since there is now more than one radio per ear (5.6 per household). The level of saturation for many consumer durables is so high that even the poorest fifth of households are well endowed with them.[10]

Consequently, the era of the household accumulation of consumer durables that sparked the growth of many manufacturing industries during the decades following World War II is largely over in the United States. Most of the future purchases of consumer durables in the United States will be for replacement and for newly established households.[11]

The point is not merely that we are reaching saturation in commodities that once defined the standard of living and quality of life, but also that the hours of labor required to obtain them have drastically declined. All in all, the commodities that used to account for over 80 percent of household consumption can now be obtained in greater abundance than previously, with less than a third of either the market or the household labor once required.[12]

Dismantling Standard Working Hours

The entry of married women into the labor force on a wide scale after World War II was a major step toward dismantling fixed daily and weekly working hours.[13] Married women often sought jobs that could be pursued part-time. And many preferred jobs that would permit them to work in blocks of time lasting several months, after which they could take several months off without losing the opportunity to return.

These new flexible arrangements are desired by an increasing number of workers, both men and women, who want a life that is not overwhelmed by earnwork. Although money and social status matter to these workers, they are content with a lifestyle that places greater emphasis on such values as family life, shared time, spiritual values, and good health. A poll conducted in late 1995 reported that 48 percent of U.S. adult earnworkers had either cut back on hours of work, declined a promotion, reduced their commitments, lowered their material expectations, or moved to a place with a quieter life during the preceding 5 years.[14] What is at issue for such employees is time – time to enjoy the things they have, time to spend with their families, time to figure out what life is all about, and time to discover the spiritual side of life.[15]

In the mid-1980s most corporations looked on nontraditional work arrangements with a jaundiced eye. Today a wide array of U.S. corporations view these alternative working arrangements as part of an inventory of personnel policies that increase corporate productivity and reduce absenteeism, labor turnover, and the cost of office space. By the second half of the 1990s, surveys were regularly reporting that top business firms had to address family and diversity issues to remain competitive in the current marketplace.[16]

Although the average annual hours of earnwork performed by household heads has continued to decline over the past quarter century, the combined hours of earnwork performed by *households* with husbands and wives present has increased by 24 percent since 1969.[17] These extra hours are concentrated in prime working ages, and they are one of the main ways that couples are financing early retirement.

What then is the virtue of increasing spending on retirement and health rather than on goods? It is the virtue of providing consumers in rich countries with what they want most. It is the virtue of not insisting that individuals must increase earnwork an extra 10 hours a week or an extra 20,000 hours per lifetime in order to produce more food or durables than they want just because such consumption will keep factories humming. The point is that leisure-time activities (including lifelong learning) – volwork – and health care are the growth industries of the twenty-first century. They will spark economic expansion during our age, just as agriculture did in the eighteenth and early nineteenth centuries and as manufacturing, transportation, and utilities did in the late nineteenth and much of the twentieth centuries.

The growing demand for health-care services is not due primarily to a distortion of the price system but to the increasing effectiveness of medical intervention. That increase since 1910 is strikingly demonstrated by comparing the second and last columns of the line on hernias in Table 2.1. Prior to World War II, hernias, when they occurred, were generally permanent and often exceedingly painful conditions. However, by the 1980s, about three-quarters of all veterans who ever had hernias were cured of them. Similar progress over the seven decades is indicated by the line on genitourinary conditions, which shows that three-quarters of those who ever had such conditions were cured of them. Other areas where medical intervention has been highly effective include control of hypertension and reduction in the incidence of stroke, surgical removal of osteoarthritis, replacement of knee and hip joints, curing of cataracts, and chemotherapies that reduce the incidence of osteoporosis and heart disease.[18] It is the success in medical interventions combined with rising incomes that has led to a huge increase in the demand for medical services.

Opportunity for Self-Realization

Today ordinary people have time to enjoy those amenities of life that only the rich could afford in abundance a century ago. These amenities broaden the mind, enrich the soul, and relieve the monotony of much of earnwork. They include travel, athletics, enjoyment of the performing arts, education, and shared time with the family.

Today people are increasingly concerned with the meaning of their lives. Earthly self-realization was not an issue for ordinary individuals in 1880, whose day was taken up almost entirely with earning money for food, clothing, and shelter, and whose reward was promised in heaven. A half century from now, perhaps even sooner, when increases in productivity make it possible to provide goods in abundance with half the labor required today, the issue of life's meaning and other matters of self-realization may take up the bulk of discretionary time.

The forecasts embodied in Tables 4.1 and 4.2 imply that by 2040 those still in the labor force, as conventionally defined, will have over 50 hours per week of leisure (volwork), that the average age of retirement (the beginning of full-time volwork or the end of regular earnwork) will begin at about age 55, and that the average duration of full-time volwork will be about 35 years.[19] Will OECD nations have the resources to afford amounts of leisure that would once have been considered luxurious and also provide high-quality health care for an additional 7 or 8 years of life?

Assuming that the per capita income of OECD nations will continue to grow at a rate of 1.5 percent per annum, the resources to finance such expanded demands will be abundant. This is a modest growth rate, well below the long-term experience since World War II and also well below the experience of the past decade and a half.[20] Consider a typical new American household established in 1995 with the head aged 20 and with the spouse earning 36 percent of the income of the head (i.e., the spouse works part time).[21] Such a household could accumulate the savings necessary to retire at age 55, with a pension paying 60 percent of its peak life-cycle earnings, by putting aside 14.7 percent of annual earning from the year that the head and spouse enter the labor force. That pension would permit retirees at age 55 to maintain their preretirement standard of living, with a real income that would rank them among the richest fifth of householders today.

By putting aside an additional 9.8 percent of income, the household can buy high-quality medical insurance that will cover the entire family until the children (two) enter the labor force, and also cover the parents' medical needs between the time they retire and age 83 (assumed to be the average age of death in their cohort). Saving an additional 7.8 percent of income will permit parents to finance the education of their children for 16 years through the bachelor's degree at a good university.[22]

What I have described is a provident fund of the type recently introduced or under consideration in some of the newly industrializing countries in Asia and Latin America.[23] I have assumed that the savings would be invested in conservatively run funds, such as the Teacher's Insurance and Annuity Association/College Retirement Equities Fund (TIAA/CREF) that is subscribed to by most American universities for their faculties. These pension funds could be managed by the government, by private firms, or as joint ventures. The only requirement is that the funds invest in a balanced portfolio of government and private securities that yield a respectable rate of return and are kept insulated from irrelevant political pressures. As in TIAA/CREF, individuals may be permitted modest latitude in choosing among investment opportunities.

The point of the example is that prospective real resources are adequate to finance early retirement, expanded high-quality education, and an increasing level of high-quality medical care (I assume that medical expenditures will increase to about 21 percent of GDP by 2040). The typical working household will still have 68 percent of a substantially larger income than is typical today to spend on other forms of consumption. Since current levels of food, clothing, and shelter will require a decreasing number of hours of work during the family's life cycle, dropping to about 20 percent of earnwork hours just before retirement, families will be able to increase their rate of accumulation in consumer durables and housing, or increase expenditure on such consumables as travel, entertainment, and education, or reduce hours of earnwork, or retire before age 55.[24]

Embedded in my simulation is a suggestion for modernizing current government systems of taxation and expenditure. Close to half of what are called taxes are actually deferred income or forced savings. In these cases, the government does not collect money for its own benefit but merely acts as an intermediary in order to ensure that money needed for later use (such as retirement) by individuals is set aside for the stated purpose and then delivered to households when needed. The particular form of intermediation exercised by the U.S. government, however, is quite peculiar. Instead of setting up an account in the name of the individual doing the savings, the government transfers the funds to a person who had earlier deferred consumption. At the same time, it promises the current taxpayer that when he or she is ready to retire, the government will find new taxpayers to provide the promised funds. Under normal circumstances, OECD governments provide this form of intermediation quite efficiently. The cost to the government of administering the U.S. Social Security system, for example, is less than six-tenths of 1 percent of expenditures.[25]

The problem with the current system, aside from the fact that it gives the impression that personal savings are actually taxes, is that its operation is subject to heavy political buffeting. As a consequence, rates of return on the savings for deferred income are highly variable and often far lower than they would have been had they been invested in a fund similar to TIAA/CREF. Moreover, the current system is affected by variations in the fertility and mortality rates that have created financial crises and thrown into doubt governments' promises that they will be able to provide the money supposedly set aside for later retirement income, health care, or education.

The crisis, then, is not in a nation's resources for providing extended retirement, improved health care, and extended education, but in the clumsy system for financing these services. The crisis is to a large extent due to accidents of history. When the original social security systems were established prior to World War I, they were intended to be class transfers. The levels of transfers were modest, supplying the elderly with barely enough food to keep them from starving. Such payments were not generally expected to cover the cost of housing or other necessities of life. Moreover, only a small percentage of a cohort was expected to live long enough to become eligible for the benefits, and the average duration of support was expected to be only a few years. Under these circumstances, a tax of 1 or 2 percent on the income of the richest 5 percent of the population was adequate to fund the program. The rich of Prussia and Great Britain were prepared to bear this cost for the sake of political stability.[26]

Over the course of the twentieth century, however, the enormous increase in life expectancy and the rising standard of living led to much longer periods of retirement and much higher levels of support after retirement. Such programs could no longer be financed through a highly concentrated class tax. To support more expensive pension systems, taxes had to be extended to the entire working population. In so doing, social security programs were transformed from redistribution schemes into systems of forced savings, although the transformation in the nature of these systems was obscure to most participants.

Modernization of the essentially self-financed programs for retirement, health care, and education from their current unsustainable systems of financing to a more transparent system of forced savings in provident funds is not easy.[27] If provident funds were being established anew, as in the case of Malaysia, no special problem would confront OECD nations. All individuals currently in the labor force would be required to set aside 32 percent of their income in a TIAA/CREF type of account to use later for the specified purposes. Although that can also be done in rich countries that currently have social insurance systems, they are confronted with the burden of meeting trillions of dollars of debt to savers under the old system. It is immoral and politically impossible to default on this obligation. Nevertheless, because of demographic factors and the unstoppable movement toward early retirement, some adjustment in the old system will have to be made.

The problem is one of intergenerational equity. It has been estimated that provident funds could be established today in the United States, and the obligations to individuals could be met under the old system, by installing a national sales tax of about 10 percent, which would continue until the last of the individuals who had paid into the old Social Security and Medicare funds had died.[28] In other words, this new tax would be greatest today and gradually diminish over the next century. A difficulty with this approach is that it places the greatest burden on the current generation. It would probably be desirable to spread this debt over several generations in order to minimize the cost of the change imposed on a particular generation. One way of spreading the burden of changing to a new system would be to borrow the funds as needed, using government securities. These securities would then be retired with taxes spread over several generations.

The problems preventing individuals from making use of the abundant resources that they have created are purely administrative. They can be solved in a manner that does not force individuals to forgo increased leisure while still in the labor force, extended retirement, expanded education for themselves and for their children, and the full benefits of modern medicine.

I have focused this analysis on the typical (median or average income) household in order to demonstrate that the economies of OECD nations have the prospective resources to permit early retirement, expanded education, and expanded medical care. Unfortunately, the income of some households is so low that saving 32 percent of earnings would not provide a provident fund large enough to permit decent retirement, health care, and education for these households. This is not a problem of inadequate national resources but of inequity. Such inequities can continue to be addressed by redistributing income from rich to poor households by taxes and subsidies. Correcting these inequities does not require restricting retirement or health care.

Self-realization requires good health and extensive leisure. The process of technophysio evolution is satisfying these conditions. Self-realization also requires, however, an answer to the question that persons with leisure have contemplated for more than 2,000 years: how do individuals realize their fullest potential? Technophysio evolution is making it possible to extend this quest from a minute fraction of the population to almost the whole of it. Although those who are retired will have more time to pursue this issue, even those still in the labor force will have sufficient leisure to seek self-realization either within their occupations or outside of them.[29]

One implication of this analysis is that decision makers both in government and in the private sector now need to review existing policies for their bearing on the timely growth of institutions that will satisfy an expanding demand for volwork. Some may consider it premature to speculate on the new forms of human activity that will come into being in order to provide solutions to the quest for self-realization. Nevertheless, I believe that one of the solutions will be lifelong education – education not to train for an occupation but to provide a better understanding of ourselves and our world. What is required is more than an expansion of existing universities and other forms of adult education. Entirely new educational forms are needed that aim at satisfying not only curiosity, but also a longing for spiritual insights that enhance the meaning of life, and that combine entertainment with edification and sociality. I believe that the desire to understand ourselves and our environment is one of the fundamental driving forces of humanity, on a par with the most basic material needs. Moreover, as per capita incomes rise and the costs of necessities and consumer durables continue to plunge, individuals and households will spend ever larger shares of their income on services that improve health, enhance knowledge, and are spiritually uplifting.[30]

Prospects for Continued Decline in the Burden of Health Care

Both environmental improvements and advances in biomedical technology contributed to a striking decline in prevalence rates of chronic conditions in high-income countries during the twentieth century. This development is illustrated for the United States by Table 4.3, which compares prevalence rates among veterans of 65 years or older around 1910 and veterans of the same ages in the mid-1980s. Even before the impact of alleviating medical intervention is considered, Table 4.3 shows that prevalence rates were down by 29 to 52 percent over the course of the seven and a half decades separating the elderly cohorts. But for two of the disorders, genitourinary conditions and central nervous system, endocrine, metabolic, and blood diseases, prevalence rates were higher in the mid-1980s than in 1910.

Medical intervention reduced prevalence rates for all six disorders. Such interventions were especially effective in chronic digestive and genitourinary disorders, where prevalence rates were cut 60 percent and 70 percent, respectively. In the cases of musculoskeletal, circulatory, and respiratory disorders, the main impact of medical intervention has been to reduce the severity of the conditions rather than to eliminate them. Whether various medical interventions cured disorders or merely attenuated them, they usually contributed to extending the duration of chronic conditions by postponing death. In other words, medical intervention appears to have had the ironic effect of increasing the duration of some disorders.

It is not yet certain whether environmental improvements and medical interventions reduced or increased the overall average duration of chronic diseases over the course of the twentieth century. Preliminary analysis indicates that the average age of onset of key

Table 4.3 Annual Rate of Decline in Prevalence Rates of Selected Chronic Conditions among Elderly Veterans between 1910 and the Mid-1980s (in Percent) before and after Alleviating Interventions

Disorders	(1) Prevalence Rates in 1910	(2) Prevalence Rates in the Mid-1980s before Alleviating Interventions	(3) Annual Rate of Decline in Prevalence Rates before Alleviating Interventions	(4) Prevalence Rates in the Mid-1980s after Alleviating Interventions	(5) Annual Rate of Decline in Prevalence Rates after Alleviating Interventions
Musculoskeletal	67.7	47.9	0.4	42.5	0.6
Digestive	84.0	49.0	0.7	18.0	2.0
Genitourinary	27.3	36.3	+0.4	8.9	1.5
Central nevous, endocrine, metabolic, or blood	24.2	29.9	+0.3	12.6	0.9
Circulatory	90.1	42.9	1.0	40.0	1.1
Respiratory	42.2	29.8	0.5	26.5	0.6

Note: + indicates an increase in prevalence rates. The term "before alleviating interventions" in Column 2 refers to interventions that alleviated existing chronic conditions, not interventions that prevented chronic conditions from occurring, as in the use of penicillin to prevent rheumatic heart disease from occurring.

Source: Table 2.1.

chronic disorders began much earlier at the beginning of the twentieth century than at the end of it among males: 11 years earlier, on average, in the cases of arthritis and respiratory disease, 9 years earlier in the case of heart disease, and 8 years earlier in the case of neoplasms.[31] But this effect is partly offset by an extension in life expectancy at age 50 of about 5 years for the elderly of the late 1980s.

Partitioning the decline in prevalence rates into environmental effects and medical intervention effects is quite complex because of the long-term effect of nutritional and other biomedical insults at earlier ages on the odds of developing chronic diseases at middle and late ages. Although such life-cycle effects have long been suspected in particular diseases, it is only recently that a substantial body of evidence bearing on the interconnections has been amassed. Longitudinal studies connecting chronic diseases at maturity, middle ages, and late ages to conditions *in utero* and infancy were reported with increasing frequency beginning in the 1980s and extending through the 1990s. The exact mechanisms by which malnutrition and trauma at early ages affect waiting time to the onset of chronic diseases are still unclear, but it seems reasonable to infer that environmental insults during the period when cell growth is rapid could lead to long-lasting impairments of vital organs.

The connections of alcohol consumption and smoking during pregnancy to the damaging of the central nervous system of fetuses were established by the early 1980s. Although suggested as early as 1968, evidence confirming that PEM could cause permanent impairment of central nervous system function accumulated in the 1990s. New evidence also indicated that iodine deficiency *in utero* and severe to moderate iron deficiency during infancy could also cause permanent neurological damage.

Perhaps the most far-reaching studies connecting early-age insults and chronic conditions at later ages were those undertaken by the Environmental Epidemiological Unit of the British Medical Research Council at the University of Southampton. Based on studies of a large sample of birth records linked to medical records at middle and late ages, they reported that such conditions as coronary heart disease, hypertension, stroke, type II diabetes, and autoimmune thyroiditis began *in utero* or in infancy but did not become apparent until mid-adult or later ages.[32] Although numerous questions were raised about the validity of these findings during the first half of the 1990s, the second half of the decade witnessed a substantial expansion of research into the connection between characteristics before age 1 year and the later onset of chronic diseases (or premature mortality), much of which confirmed the original studies.[33]

The theory of a nexus between environmental insults *in utero* or at early ages and the onset of chronic diseases at later ages suggests that the rapid advances in public health technology between 1890 and 1950 should contribute to a continuing decline in the prevalence rates of chronic diseases and perhaps even to an acceleration of this decline. The first half of the twentieth century witnessed an avalanche of new technologies that improved the environment, including the cleaning up of the water and milk supplies, the widespread draining of swamps, the improvement of garbage disposal and sewage systems, the rapid reduction in the use of animals (especially in cities) for transportation, the switch to electricity and to fuels with a lower carbon content than had been used previously, and the rapid advance in obstetric technology and neonatal care. This period also witnessed significant improvements in the diversity of the food supply throughout the year and the beginning of dietary supplements that improved year-round consumption of vitamins and other trace elements.

Evidence that the rate of decline in chronic and disabling conditions may be accelerating has been reported by the investigators at the Center for Demographic Studies at Duke University who have made use of data obtained from National Long-Term Care Surveys conducted between 1982 and 1999. This study reported an average annual decline of about 1.7 percent in disability rates during the 17-year period. However, when this period was broken into three parts, there was a statistically significant acceleration in the rate of decline during the second and third parts of the period as compared with the first part. The study attributes the acceleration to a variety of health and socioeconomic factors, including the level of education, which increased markedly and rapidly during the first half of the twentieth century.[34]

Does the mounting evidence of the long-term decline in the prevalence rate of chronic diseases, and what also may be an acceleration in the long-term rate of decline, mean that the "supply" of treatable chronic diseases is declining? I use the word "supply" in order to distinguish the physiological burden of health care from the demand for health care services, which may rise even if the physiological burden remains constant or declines. Moreover, I use a different definition of the burden of disease than that employed by the WHO and the World Bank.[35] They treat death as the maximum burden of disease, as it should be from an ethical standpoint. However, from a financial standpoint, death terminates health care expenditures on a particular individual. Consequently, to address the question of whether declines in physiological prevalence rates will relieve current fiscal pressures on the health care systems of OECD nations, it is necessary to weight the existence of a particular chronic disease by the cost of treating that condition, which generally increases with age.

Such an index is shown in Figure 4.1. In this figure the burden of per capita health care costs, which is based on U.S. data, is standardized at 100 for ages 50–54. Figure 4.1 shows that the financial burden of health care per capita rises slowly in the 50s, accelerates in the 60s, accelerates again in the 70s, and accelerates even more rapidly after the mid-80s. The financial per capita burden at age 85 and over is nearly six times as high as the burden at ages 50–54. Notice that the financial burden of health care at ages 85 and above is over 75 percent higher per capita than at ages 75–79. However, the physiological prevalence rate (number of conditions per person) is roughly constant at ages 80 and over.

Costs rise, even though the number of conditions per person remains constant, because the severity of the conditions increases or because the cost of preventing further deterioration, or even partially reversing deterioration, increases with age. It should be kept in mind that standard prevalence rates merely count the number

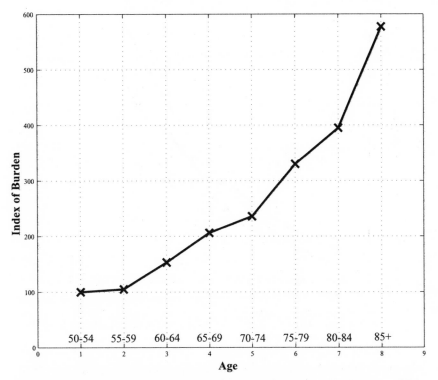

Figure 4.1 Relative Burden of Health Care by Age, U.S. Data c. 1996 (average burden of 50- to 54-year-olds = 100).

Sources: Fogel 2000, Table 5D.1; Federal Interagency Forum on Aging-Related Statistics 2000, Table 26B.

of conditions, neglecting both the increasing physiological deterioration with age and the rising cost of treatment per condition. Figure 4.1 indicates that to forecast the future financial burden of health care, it is necessary to make use of a function of the age-specific cost of health care, such as that shown in Figure 4.1. It is also necessary to adjust for the changing age structure of the population and the changing specific cost at each age.

What, then, can be said about the likely movements in the curve of the relative burden of health care costs at ages 50 and over during the next generation? Figure 4.2 lays out three possibilities. The first possibility is that there will be a proportional downward shift in

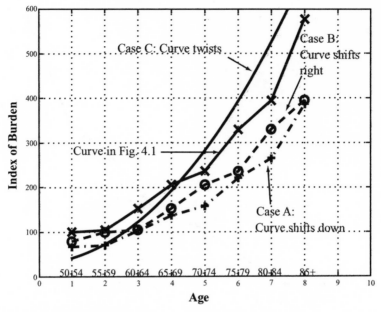

Figure 4.2 How Will the Curve of Relative Disease Burden Shift?

the curve (Case A). This is the curve implied by using the change in the average prevalence rate, which implies a shift downward at a constant average rate at all ages. The example shown in Figure 4.2 implies a decline in average prevalence rates of 1.2 percent per annum,[36] which locates all of the points in Case A at about two-thirds of the previous level. If I had used 1.5 percent, the points on the Case A curve would all be located at about 60 percent of the original level.

A second alternative, shown as Case B in Figure 4.2, is that the curve of disease burden by age will shift to the right. The Case B curve was constructed on the assumption that over the course of a generation the average age of onset of chronic conditions is delayed by about 5 years. This assumption is supported by a number of epidemiological studies in the Netherlands, Britain, the United States, and elsewhere. This forecast is based partly on the evidence that the average age of the onset of chronic disabilities has been declining since the start of the twentieth century.

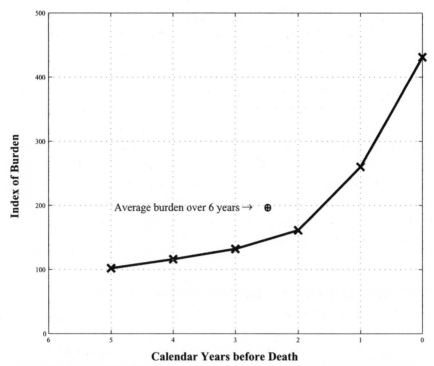

Figure 4.3 Index of Average Annual Health Care Costs by Year before Death.

It is also based on studies of the relative cost of health care by years before death. These studies have produced the curve shown in Figure 4.3, which is standardized on the average costs of health care for all persons age 65 and over in the U.S. Medicare program. Figure 4.3 shows that 5 years before the year of death, the annual health cost is virtually the same as all annual Medicare costs per capita. By the second year before death the cost has risen by about 60 percent, and in the year of death the annual cost exceeds the average by over four times. Indeed, expenditures on persons during their last 2 years of life account for 40 percent of all Medicare expenditures.

The pattern portrayed in Figure 4.3 has not changed signifi-cantly over the past two decades. The relative constancy in health care costs by years before death supports Case B in Figure 4.2, since it implies that no matter how far to the right the health care curve shifts, age-specific costs will eventually rise sharply as the proportion of persons who die in any given age category increases.

Figure 4.2 shows a third possibility, Case C. In that case, the curve of age-specific health costs twists. At ages 50 through 64 the curve shifts downward, while at ages above 65 the curve rises. The downward shift before age 65 is due to a presumed acceleration in the delay in the onset of chronic diseases and an initially slower rate of deterioration. The sharper rise after age 65 is due partly to a diffusion of the most expensive interventions and partly to the assumption that the more effective interventions of the future will also be more expensive.

Forecasting Trends in the Demand for Health Care Services

So far, I have focused purely on the economic burden of treatable chronic conditions. Figures 4.1 and 4.2 focused on the cost-adjusted supply of treatable conditions. I now want to consider the likely trend in the demand for health care services by consumers. Table 4.4 presents the change in the structure of consumption in the United States between 1875 and 1995. The trend in the structure of consumption in other OECD nations has been quite similar. The term "expanded consumption" takes account of the fact that as income has increased, consumers have preferred to take an increasing share of their real income in the form of leisure rather than in purchasing more commodities, as would be possible if they did not reduce their hours of work.

One notable feature of Table 4.4 is the change in the share of income spent on food, clothing, and shelter, which has declined from 74 percent of expanded consumption to just 13 percent over the 120-year period. Another striking change is the share of income spent on health care, which has increased nine-fold, from 1 percent of expenditures to 9 percent.

Table 4.4 The Long-Term Trend in the Structure of Consumption and the Implied Income Elasticities of Several Consumption Categories

Consumption Class	Distribution of Consumption (%)		Long-Term Income Elasticities
	1875	*1995*	
Food	49	5	0.2
Clothing	12	2	0.3
Shelter	13	6	0.7
Health care	1	9	1.6
Education	1	5	1.6
Other	6	7	1.1
Leisure	18	68	1.5

Source: Fogel 2000.

For purposes of forecasting, the most important feature of Table 4.4 is the last column, which presents the long-term income elasticities for each category of expenditures. The "income elasticity" is defined as the percentage increase in expenditures on a given commodity that will occur with a 1 percent increase in income. Notice that the income elasticities for food and clothing are quite low, which means that the share of these items in total consumption will continue to decline. An income elasticity of 1 means that the share of a given item in total consumption will remain constant. Notice that shelter, which includes most consumer durables, is closer to but still below 1. On the other hand, the income elasticities for health care, education, and leisure are all well above 1. The income elasticity of 1.6 means that income expenditures on health care in the United States are likely to rise from a current level of about 14 percent of GDP to about 21 percent of GDP in 2040.

Is that bad? Should such a development be avoided? Should governments seek to thwart consumer demand for health care services? Such a policy would be necessary only if OECD nations lacked the resources to provide that much health care. However, the growth in productivity of traditional commodities, including food, clothing, shelter, and consumer durables, will release the resources required to provide expanded health care. In the United States a century ago, it took about 1,700 hours of work to purchase the annual food supply for a family. Today it requires just 260 hours. If agricultural productivity grows at just two-thirds of its recent rates, then by 2040 a family's annual food supply may be purchased with about 160 hours of labor.

A recent study of the role of the change in the benefits and costs of health care conducted by investigators at the National Bureau of Economic Research (NBER) concluded that the benefits of health care services over the past 40 years have more than justified their costs. This analysis suggests a fundamental repositioning of the public debate about medical care from how governments can limit spending to how to get the most out of the spending that is undertaken.[37] Other NBER investigators have also suggested changing the methods of health care financing so that the consumer demand for increasingly effective services is not unnecessarily thwarted.[38]

Forecasting Health Care Costs in China and Other Third World Countries

A number of factors suggest that health costs will rise more rapidly as a percentage of national income among Third World nations that are now entering into modern economic growth than has been the case in OECD countries. Some of these factors are on the supply side, while others are on the demand side. My argument can be illustrated by considering the case of China.

The supply of chronic conditions that require treatment is much greater at middle and late ages in China than the supply that currently exists in OECD nations. This heavy burden of chronic diseases is due partly to the remarkable rate of increase in life expectancy since 1950. Life expectancy in China in 1950 was only 41 years at birth, which means that the infant death rate was close

Table 4.5 Average Number of Chronic Conditions per U.S. Male in 1900 and in the 1990s

Age	c. 1900	1992–96	Average Annual Rate of Decline (%)
50–54	3.3	1.0	1.3
55–59	4.5	1.4	1.2
60–64	5.6	1.6	1.3
65–69	6.2	1.9	1.3

Sources: For 1900, the Union Army Data Set collected by the Center for Population Economics at the University of Chicago (see http://www.cpe.uchicago.edu); for 1992–96, the Health and Retirement Study surveys (see http://hrsonline.isr.umich.edu/).

to 200 per thousand.[39] Such a low life expectancy and such a high infant death rate mean that those who survived to middle ages experienced severe biomedical and socioeconomic insults *in utero*, in infancy, and in later developmental ages. Despite the rapid advances in public health and strong economic growth, the negative conditions that influenced physiological development remained severe into the early 1960s. As I have already pointed out, such early-life insults reduce the waiting time to the onset of chronic diseases at later ages and increase their severity.

Consequently, individuals who are age 50 and older in China today will have far higher prevalence rates of chronic diseases than is the case in OECD nations. One would have to go back at least to the beginning of the twentieth century in OECD countries to approximate the burden of chronic diseases in China today. This point is illustrated by Table 4.5, which shows the average number of chronic conditions per person in the United States at middle and later ages at both the beginning and the end of the twentieth century. In 1900 there were about three times as many chronic conditions per person on average at ages 50–54 as there were in the mid-1990s. Roughly the same proportion exists in the other age intervals shown in Table 4.5. By ages 65–69 the average American male in 1900 suffered from more than six chronic conditions, many of which were severely debilitating.

Table 4.6 Average Capacity of Males
to Engage in Manual Labor, by Age,
c. 1900 (percentages)

Age	Capacity to Engage in Manual Labor
50–54	0.75
55–59	0.56
60–64	0.34
65–69	0.17
70–74	0.08
75 and over	0.04

Note: Capacity at prime ages = 100.
Source: Union Army Data Set collected by the
Center for Population Economics at the University
of Chicago (see http://www.cpe.uchicago.edu).

Just how debilitating the epidemiological regime is in poor countries is indicated by Table 4.6. This table reports the average capacity of American men to engage in manual labor at the beginning of the twentieth century. If we take work capacity between ages 25 and 29 to be 100 percent, by ages 50–54 the capacity to engage in manual labor had dropped to 75 percent. By ages 60 to 64, work capacity was only a third of the peak. After age 70, work capacity was less than 10 percent of the peak. Of course, a low capacity to work means considerable suffering from a variety of chronic conditions. So the process of aging under conditions of poverty means not only that individuals have multiple disabilities, but also that these conditions are extremely debilitating.

By itself, a large supply of disabilities does not create a high level of demand for health care. In order for the demand for health care to be high, income has to be high. Individuals do not spend large amounts on health care when nearly all of their income must be devoted to food, clothing, and shelter. In the United States during the late nineteenth century, when chronic conditions were much more widespread than they are today and the severity of these conditions was much greater than it is today, less than 2 percent of income was spent on health care. Today, however, despite much lower age-specific prevalence rates of chronic conditions, the United States spends some 14 percent of GDP on health care.[40]

The experience of OECD nations suggests that health care costs will rise more rapidly in China as a share of GDP than they did in OECD countries. A higher rate of growth in health care costs would be expected even if the income elasticity of demand in China is the same as it has been in OECD countries. If, for example, China's GDP grows at 8 percent per annum between 2000 and 2030, the share of health care services in GDP would rise from under 3 percent to about 8.5 percent during the same period.

It is likely, however, that the income elasticity of the demand for health care will be somewhat higher in China during these three decades than it has been in OECD countries. I base this forecast partly on the rapid rate of increase in urbanization that can be expected in China over the three decades. The changing proportion of the population living in cities will raise the demand for health care for a number of reasons. First, traditional medicine is preferred in rural regions, while Western medicine is preferred in the cities; the cost of Western medicine per user is much higher than the cost of traditional medicine. Consequently, the change in the share of the population living in cities will increase the total cost of medical care more rapidly than the growth of demand for medical care within each of the two geographical sectors taken separately.

Second, the rate of change in biomedical technology is very rapid and accelerating. So far, technological change in Western medicine has tended to increase its cost rather than reduce it. Although some procedures, such as coronary bypass operations, are somewhat cheaper than they used to be, many procedures are more expensive. Individuals are willing to accept more expensive procedures because they are also usually more effective. Indeed, the rapid decline in the price of chip-making has made it possible to design new mechanisms that could not have been considered with the older technology but that, for this reason, are more expensive.

China is still early in the process of investing in consumer durables. The penetration level of automobiles is still a very small percentage of all households. However, the penetration of other consumer durables, such as refrigerators and television sets, is nearing 80 percent. As households achieve their objectives with respect to consumer durables, the share of income spent on health care will increase. In this connection, it should be kept in mind that the income level of households in big cities is relatively high by international standards. For example, per capita income in the 14 open coastal cities is more than three and a half times the national per capita income. Put on an international scale, using purchasing-power parity (PPP), the average per capita income of these cities in 1999 was about $11,700.00.[41] Hence, the average household in these large cities has an income equal to that of the richest countries in the category that the World Bank classifies as upper middle income. At such levels of income – as high, for example, as those of Argentina, Chile, Greece, or the Czech Republic – pressures on the health care system become similar to those that exist in OECD nations. Hence, if the growth of cities with more than 1 million people is more rapid than the growth of smaller cities, that will be an additional factor promoting an income elasticity of the demand for health care that is greater than 1.6.

Three other factors that will tend to stimulate the growth of the demand for health care should be mentioned. One is the increasing level of education. Another is the increasing use of the computer and the Internet. A third is the growth of insurance companies, which is being accelerated by China's entry into the World Trade Organization (WTO). All three of these developments promote knowledge of the effectiveness of the high-tech procedures in Western medicine and increase the demand for them. Moreover, the speed at which the newest, and generally the more expensive, procedures and drugs become known will tend to be even greater in the future.

Still another factor promoting the demand for health care services is the growth of the population and the change in age composition. During the next 30 years, the population of China will increase by about 27 percent and the proportion of the population over age 50 (the age at which the prevalence rate of chronic conditions begins to accelerate rapidly) will increase from 19 percent to 34 percent.[42]

Public policy should not be aimed at suppressing the demand for health care. Expenditures on health care are driven by demand, which is spurred by income and by advances in biotechnology that make health interventions increasingly effective. Just as electricity and manufacturing were the industries that stimulated the growth of the rest of the economy at the beginning of the twentieth century, health care is the growth industry of the twenty-first century. It is a leading sector, which means that expenditures on health care will pull forward a wide array of other industries including manufacturing, education, financial services, communications, and construction.

The pressure to suppress health care expenditures arises from the way that governments and businesses currently provide insurance in both OECD countries and China. These institutions need to provide a basic and affordable package of health services. Beyond that, they should offer additional policies at higher costs that provide upscale services (such as private rooms, the most expensive alternative procedures and medicines, the shortest waiting time, the fullest coverage of optional services, and access to physicians anywhere in the country, not just in local clinics). Health care is not a homogeneous good, all of which is essential. There are large luxury components in health services that may appeal to some tastes but that are not necessary for sound basic health care. It is, of course, necessary to provide medical care for those who are too poor to purchase it from their own resources, but for those with more resources, shifting to private savings accounts for health services is an effective way to relieve pressure on the finances of both businesses and government.

5

Problems of Equity in Health Care

In the United States and around the world, concern is growing about who gets health care. Individuals from different socioeconomic backgrounds face distressingly different prospects of living a healthy life. As numerous studies confirm, the disparities in various measures of health between the privileged and the deprived still remain wide, even in rich countries, despite the long-term tendency toward a healthier society.[1]

Some investigators believe that the disparities are actually increasing. They suggest that the shift in the health care system in advanced industrial countries from the principle of universal access to a more market-oriented system may be one cause of the growing disparities they observe; rising income inequality is another potential culprit.

Policy makers worldwide meanwhile speak of more efficiently delivering "essential" health care, but nobody is certain what this means in practice.

What counts as essential in health care? What is the optimal mix of private and government components of health care services? To answer these questions, it is necessary to confront the question of how to define essential health care and then explore the policy implications of the analysis.

Standards for Rationing

International organizations such as WHO and the OECD have called on all countries to guarantee delivery of "high-quality essential care to all persons, defined mostly by criteria of effectiveness, cost and social acceptability."[2] Cost has become a controlling issue since the health care systems established in most OECD countries after World War II, which sought to guarantee complete health care for all through government-run health or insurance systems, have become so expensive that they now threaten the fiscal stability of governments. As incomes rose, the public demand for health services increased much more rapidly than income (because of the high income elasticity of the demand for health care), making the cost of operating such systems unsustainable.

The new systems of essential care now being developed in OECD countries recognize the necessity of explicitly establishing priorities among health interventions (rather than unlimited coverage), which means that it has become necessary to ration health care services much more tightly than was previously conceded. In order to guarantee that the health of the poor is not neglected under the new system, WHO proposes three principles: health care services should be prepaid (i.e., taxes for health care should be collected throughout the working life, even though the need for services is relatively low during young adult and middle ages); those who are healthy should subsidize those who are sick (which means that taxes should not be adjusted to reflect differential health risks, as policy rates often are under private insurance); and the rich should subsidize the poor (which means both that the rich should pay higher health taxes than the poor and that the quality of service in government-run programs should be no better or more comprehensive for privileged groups).[3]

This recommended standard explicitly recognizes that privately funded health programs and private insurance will need to provide a major part of a nation's health services. Since persons in the upper half of income distributions tend to spend more on health services than poorer people do, the distribution of health services is bound to be unequal. In fact, all OECD countries currently have mixed private and governmental systems, ranging from about 85 percent of total expenditures made by the government in Great Britain to about 45 percent in the United States.[4] It is likely that the reforms now in progress will generally increase the private share of health care services.

There is no clear agreement currently on the optimal mix of private and government components of health care services. There is not much literature on this question, nor is there a consensus on the criteria that should be invoked to resolve the issue. Moreover, conditions vary so much from country to country that the optimal mix cannot be the same for all countries.

In very poor countries, where the need for health care services is great, the average annual level of per capita expenditures from both sources is shockingly low. In such countries as Ethiopia, Haiti, Indonesia, and Nepal, annual per capita expenditures range between $20 and $56 (using international dollars, which adjust exchange rates for the domestic purchasing power of a country's currency). In India the figure is a still a very low $84, and in China it is $74. By contrast, the figures for the five largest countries of Western Europe are: Germany $2,365, France $2,135, Italy $1,824, Spain $1,211, and the United Kingdom $1,193. Annual per capita expenditures in the United States on health care, $3,724, are more than 3 times the British figure and more than 1.5 times the German figure. The spending of the typical American in 10 days exceeds the average *annual* expenditures of people living in countries with more than three-fifths of the world's population.

The fact that Europeans spend so much less on health care than Americans has led some critics to argue that the American system is wasteful. This contention is often buttressed by the fact that American disability-adjusted life expectancy at birth is less than that of France, Spain, Italy, the United Kingdom, and Germany. If all those extra dollars spent by Americans are not buying better health and longer lives, what are they buying?

It is not yet possible to provide an adequate answer to that question. It is often assumed that the increase in longevity over the past two or three decades is due primarily to the increased amount and quality of health care services. There is no doubt that medical interventions have saved many lives, especially in such areas as infectious diseases, cancer, and heart disease. However, we cannot yet say how much of the 6 or so years of increased life expectancy since 1970 is due to medical interventions and how much is due to better levels of education, improvements in housing, and other factors that contribute to the increase in life expectancy.

Some recent findings suggest that most of the huge increase in life expectancy since 1900 is due to the large investment in public health programs between 1880 and World War II that cleaned up the water and milk supplies, developed modern waste disposal systems, reduced air pollution, and improved the nutritional status.[5] Of course, these public health programs were prompted by advances in medical knowledge. But the research behind these public health advances represents a relatively small part of what is included in the category of health expenditures. In the United States, for example, medical research (not including research and development [R&D] of drug companies and providers of medical equipment and supplies) adds up to just 1.7 percent of national health expenditures.

Since deaths due to infectious diseases are now a small proportion of total deaths, it might seem that environmental improvements that were so important in reducing health risks before 1950 have been exhausted. Such a conclusion is premature. A series of recent studies has reported a connection between exposure to stress (biological and social) in early life, including insults *in utero* and during infancy, with the onset of chronic diseases at middle and late ages and with reduced life expectancy. The strongest evidence for such links that has emerged thus far is with respect to hypertension, coronary heart disease, and type II diabetes.[6] A review of

32 papers dealing with the relationship between birth weight and hypertension showed a tendency for blood pressure to increase in middle age as birth weight declined.[7] Evidence of a connection between birth size and later coronary heart disease has been found in England, Wales, Sweden, India, and Finland.[8] The number of studies confirming the impact of insults during developmental ages on health in later life has increased substantially since 1994.[9]

One of the strongest recent confirmations of the impact of early life events on longevity is a study reporting a statistically significant relationship between longevity after age 50 and week of birth for cohorts born between 1863 and 1918. In the Northern Hemisphere, average length of life is shortest for those born in the second quarter of the year and longest for those born in the fourth quarter. In Australia, the relationship between birth month and longevity exists but the peak and trough are the mirror image of those in the Northern Hemisphere.[10] This result, which is apparently related to seasonal variations in nutritional status, has also been found in the American data for cohorts born between 1820 and 1850.[11] Consequently, we cannot rule out the proposition that one of the biggest factors influencing the prevalence rates of the chronic diseases among the elderly in 2001 (and which accounts for a huge slice of national medical expenditures) was their exposure to environmental insults half a century or more ago.

These new scientific findings are directly relevant to the problem of how to define essential health care and how to divide the national budget for health (regardless of how it is financed) among competing needs. It may well be that a very large increase in expenditures on antenatal care and pediatric care in infancy and early childhood is the most effective way to improve health over the entire life cycle by delaying the onset of chronic diseases, alleviating their severity if they do occur, and increasing longevity.

Whatever the virtues of such a strategy, it raises the issue of intergenerational bias. This strategy gives a preference to the unborn and the very young over the immediate needs of the elderly. It is a double blow to the elderly, who are now suffering from the early onset of chronic conditions and premature disability because of environmental insults they incurred *in utero* and in early childhood. Yet, under a strategy that emphasizes antenatal and early childhood care, in order to make new generations better off throughout their life cycles, the elderly of today will be asked to restrain their demand for relief.

It is much easier to define essential care in the impoverished nations of the world, because their alternatives are so stark. They are still suffering from killing and crippling diseases, virtually eliminated from OECD nations, that can be vanquished at quite modest costs compared to the expensive procedures routinely used to deal with more moderate complaints in rich countries. The prospects of the poorest billion in the Third World can be "radically improved by targeting a relatively small set of diseases and conditions."[12]

The urgent needs include the distribution of drugs to combat tuberculosis, malaria, and acute gastrointestinal and respiratory infections; vaccines to prevent measles, tetanus, and diphtheria; and improved nutrition to revitalize immune systems, reduce perinatal deaths, lower death rates from a wide range of infectious diseases, and improve the functioning of the central nervous system. The Commission on Macroeconomics and Health (CMH) of WHO has estimated that 87 percent of deaths among children under age 5, 71 percent of deaths between ages 5 and 29, and 47 percent of deaths between ages 30 and 69 can be avoided by making use of available drugs and vaccines, by the delivery of vital nutrients, and by public health programs aimed at producing safe water supplies, improved sanitation, and improved health education.[13] CMH estimates that donations from private and public sources in OECD countries, amounting to just 0.14 percent of their combined GDP, will be enough to achieve these objectives rapidly.[14]

Defining essential health care for the United States is more problematic because the technologies needed for rapid and dramatic improvements in health and longevity are still on the drawing board, in contrast to poor countries, where the problem is how to deliver effectively known health technologies. To clarify the issue of essential care in a country where per capita expenditures on health exceed those of poor nations by 50 to 150 times, it is necessary to consider exactly what it is that our luxurious (even by European standards) expenditures are buying.

Saving lives, as important as it is and as effective at it as modern medicine has become, is not the main activity of physicians and other health professionals. As I have already indicated, it is likely that past public health reforms, improvements in nutrition and other living standards, and the democratization of education have done much more to increase longevity than has clinical medicine. The main thing that physicians do is to make life more bearable: to relieve pain, to reduce the severity of chronic conditions, to postpone disabilities or even overcome some of them, to mend broken limbs, to prescribe drugs, and to reduce anxiety, overcome depression, and instruct individuals on how to take care of themselves.

Europeans are much more willing than Americans to stint on unnecessary services, on procedures that are optional rather than vital, on conveniences rather than necessities, on small rather than large reductions in risk, and on wide choice rather than limited choice or no choice (take it or leave it). Consider the issue of queuing, one of the principal devices employed by public health systems in Europe to keep demand from exceeding politically negotiated budgets. Americans are unwilling to wait 2 years or more for a hernia operation, as is now the case in Britain, but demand that such a service be available quickly, in a few weeks in most cases.[15] Americans chafe at another favorite European device to control costs: rationing. They do not want to be told that they are too old or too fit or not fit enough to be eligible for some course of treatment. Nor are they willing to have their access to specialists sharply curtailed, and so the ratio of specialists to primary care physicians is much higher in the United States than elsewhere. They also resist hasty, impersonal examinations and denial of access to inpatient hospital care.[16] And the rich insist on being allowed to spend as much on health care as they desire, even if some of these expenditures are wasteful.

And so the United States has some 6,000 hospitals, while Britain's National Health Service has only 430 very large hospitals (beds per capita are similar in both countries).[17] Every substantial suburban community in the United States demands its own facility with a wide range of services. Today, not just research hospitals but also many community hospitals have on staff physicians who specialize in heart bypass surgery and other high-tech procedures. Since Americans like to save a buck as much as Europeans, they are willing to join health maintenance organizations (HMOs), but HMOs have found that to be competitive, they have to offer numerous options on co-payments, access to physicians outside of the primary network, and self-referral to specialists. Americans also demand the option to change health plans if they are dissatisfied. Such options cost money because, among other things, they increase the cost of administration, even if they do not improve health outcomes.[18]

The American passion for such individually tailored health services may be attributed to American culture: the wide-open spaces, evangelical religion, and hostility to government. But it also reflects income. The average American, after all, is 50 percent richer than the average British person. Hence, it is not strange that they are willing to consume services that are too expensive for poorer people. Americans are no more self-indulgent in their purchases of health care than they are in their purchases of appliances or cars.[19]

And so, what is viewed as essential health care in the United States includes items that in other cultures would be regarded as wasteful luxuries. This misunderstanding of the American system is relevant to the proposition that 15 percent of Americans are uncovered by health insurance. "Uncovered" does not mean that they are untreated. The uninsured see doctors almost as frequently as the insured. Nor is it clear that the effectiveness of their care is always less than that of those who have insurance. The uninsured are treated in public clinics and in emergency rooms, which (although they lack the conveniences of insured care and may have long queues) provide competent services, both standard and high tech.[20]

Although access to health care matters, insurance alone does not guarantee adequate access. Moreover, while some of the uninsured in the U.S. system are in poorer health than the insured, others are in prime ages, have relatively good health, and prefer to self-insure. An important but poorly addressed issue is how different attitudes toward risk influence the insured and the uninsured in deciding when and where to seek health care. This issue is important when considering solutions for those who are underserved in health care, since underservice of the poor also exists in countries with universal health insurance.[21] If the poor and the young are willing to accept higher health risks than are the rich and the elderly, merely extending entitlements may not be adequate. An aggressive outreach program, targeted at those who fail to take advantage of entitlements, may be required.

Priorities for Reform

The best way to improve the health system for the poor is to identify their most urgent needs and design an effective way of ministering to those specific needs. This goal will not be met merely by equalizing the annual number of visits to doctors (since the rich often waste medical services) or the annual expenditures on drugs (since the rich often overmedicate). Focusing on the specific needs of the poor may not save money, but it will ensure that whatever is spent is properly targeted.

In this spirit, the number one priority ought to be an expansion of prenatal and postnatal care targeted particularly at young, single mothers. This priority is suggested by the new evidence that proper nutrition, including supplements of such key nutrients as folate and iron, can reduce perinatal deaths and birth defects, including damage to the central nervous system. It is also necessary to counsel pregnant women on the dangers to the fetus of smoking and alcohol consumption, and on the benefits of proper diets, regular and early examinations, and exposing the fetus to a stimulating environment (music and conversation). A focus on young, single mothers makes sense not only because they are among the most needy, but also because there is now persuasive evidence that insults *in utero* that reduce birth weight and length, as well as inadequate weight gains in infancy, greatly increase health risks throughout the life cycle.

A second priority is improved health education and mentoring to enable poorly educated people, both young and old, to identify their health problems, to follow instructions for health care, to use medication properly, and to become involved in social networks conducive to good health. It not enough to wait for such individuals to seek out available services. Outreach programs need to be developed to identify the needy individuals. Hence, support should be extended to organizations already experienced in outreach, such as the Girls Clubs of America and community churches, so that they can include health screening and counseling among their services. Systems for monitoring the effectiveness of such community organizations also need to be established.

Another priority is the reintroduction into public schools, particularly those in poor neighborhoods, from nursery school through the 12th grade, of periodic health screening programs, using nurses and physicians on a contract basis. Personnel should also be employed to ensure that parents understand the nature of their children's problems and to direct the parents to public health facilities that can provide appropriate services.

A fourth initiative is the establishment of public health clinics in underserved poor neighborhoods that can supplement the emergency rooms of regular hospitals, which are a frequent source of routine health care services for the poor and near poor.[22] Convenient access is a key issue, since even individuals with insurance, such as those on Medicaid, fail to take advantage of available facilities because they are inconvenient. Time is a cost to the poor as well as the rich, and a lack of convenient facilities may cause individuals to accept higher health risks than they would otherwise choose. The mission of community clinics should include health education in addition to treatment. Community clinics need to be regularly monitored to ensure their effectiveness. Church basements and public schools after normal teaching hours can be good locations for community clinics both because they help to stretch available funds and because they provide familiar settings.

Readers may be surprised that I have not emphasized the extension of health insurance policies to the 15 percent of the population not currently insured. The flap over insurance has more to do with taxation than with health services. Keep in mind that the poor are already entitled to health care under Medicaid and that the near poor often receive free health care through county or city hospitals and emergency rooms. What they do not do is pay taxes for those services. Most proposals for extending health insurance involve taxing their wages for services they already receive. Such insurance may relieve the pressure on the public purse, but it will not guarantee better health care. I believe that health screening in schools and community clinics has a better chance at success than unexercised theoretical entitlements.

Finally, any consideration of how to reduce health inequality must involve a reconsideration of America's obligation to increase its contribution to the international campaign to bring vaccines and other products to children and adults whose lives can be saved if there is the international will to do so. The lack of access to such products in the poorest 50 or so countries is the most glaring instance of inequality in the global health system and a lingering threat to the health of those in rich countries.

The large advances in life expectancy in China and other emerging economies show that it is not necessary to wait for industrialization to be completed before making major advances in health and longevity. Modern methods of sanitation and other public health programs can be introduced at a modest cost. Cleaning up the water supply, improving the distribution of basic nutrients, draining swamps and otherwise disrupting vectors of disease, and improving waste disposal can be achieved quickly and cheaply, as has been demonstrated by China, Indonesia, and Malaysia.[23] OECD nations can help speed up the process in countries still lagging behind by training public health officials, by helping to supply vital nutrients to pregnant mothers and infants, and by helping to supply antibiotics and other vital drugs and vaccines.

A particularly urgent issue is posed by the worldwide pandemic of human immunodeficiency virus/acquired immune deficiency syndrome (HIV/AIDS). Although death rates from AIDS have recently declined in the United States and other OECD nations, AIDS is ravaging Africa. Of the 3 million individuals worldwide who died of AIDS in 2000, more than 2 million lived in sub-Saharan Africa.[24] Although rates of infection are still relatively low in India and China, they are at risk of a rapid escalation in the spread of the infection. Public campaigns to inform the populations of these countries of the threat of this disease, of means of reducing the odds of infection, and of available treatment for those already infected are urgently needed. OECD and international agencies can provide both money and skilled personnel to confront AIDS and other deadly infectious diseases, and to help provide vaccines and other drug therapies to those who need them. One important way to help is by increasing the R&D budgets of the OECD nations for diseases that afflict the poor countries of the world. It is not only morality but also self-interest that argues for these measures. Epidemics in the Third World can spread to OECD nations.

The current concern with making the distribution of health care more equal reflects both the large increase of global per capita income during the twentieth century and the great strides in biomedical technology. To poor people, adequate food takes precedence over seeing a doctor. As the people in OECD nations escaped poverty, they demanded more and more health care. The same pattern is now apparent in many Third World countries. The increasing share of global income spent on health care expenditures is not a calamity; it is a sign of the remarkable social and economic progress of our age.

Postscript

How Long Can We Live?

W ill the twenty-first century witness as large an increase in the average life expectancy of the rich countries – thirty to forty years – as occurred during the twentieth century? Most experts believe it will not. The middle estimate of the U.S. Census Bureau, for example, is that the increase in life expectancy between 2000 and 2050 will be only about 7 years, and the estimated increase for the entire twenty-first century is just 13 years. This is less than half the increase that occurred during the twentieth century. The same conservatism is evident in the projections of the UN, OECD, and other national and international agencies.[1]

These pessimistic projections rest on several propositions. Perhaps the most widely accepted is the proposition that opportunities for large reductions in mortality rates are possible only when death rates under age 5 are very high. Proponents of this view argue, for example, that the sharp decline in U.S. mortality rates during the twentieth century was the result of a unique opportunity that cannot be replicated by those nations that have already experienced it: the opportunity to wipe out the majority of deaths due to acute infectious diseases, which were concentrated in infancy and early childhood. Whereas more than a third of all deaths at the turn of the twentieth century were of children under 5, today infant and childhood deaths are less than 2 percent of the annual total. By contrast, deaths among persons age 65 and over, which accounted for just 18 percent of the total in 1900, have grown to three-quarters of all deaths today.[2]

Thus, at the start of the twenty-first century, the argument goes, the more than 90 percent of birth cohorts who live to age 50 begin to suffer from an increasing number of chronic diseases because their vital organ systems naturally lose their effectiveness with aging, and this deterioration eventually increases to a point where life can no longer be sustained. Empirical observations are buttressed by a variety of theories, some of them drawn from evolutionary biology, as to why the cells of vital organ systems decay. One prominent theory holds that because reproduction ceases at age 50, there is a sharp rise in deaths at postreproductive ages because the forces of natural selection have not eliminated the genes that hasten rapid physiological decline past age 50.

There are, however, persuasive arguments that spell out a more optimistic view of the course of changes in health and longevity during the twenty-first century. One of these arguments is based on the projection not of past changes in *average* life expectancy but of *record* life expectancy since 1840. Record life expectancy is defined as the highest life expectancy experienced by any country at each point in time. For example, the record life expectancy at birth in 1840 was found among Swedish women, who lived on average a bit over 45 years. In the year 2000, Japanese women achieved a record life expectancy of nearly 85 years. Fitting a curve to such best practice observations over a period of 160 years yields a linear curve, which suggests that for the foreseeable future, female life expectancy will increase at 2.4 years per decade and male life expectancy will increase at 2.2 years per decade. These equations lead to the prediction that by 2070 female life expectancy in the United States will be between 92.5 and 101.5 years, which substantially exceeds the forecast of 83.9 years made by the Social Security Administration in 1999.[3]

The fact is that demographers' past predictions of maximum life expectancy have been notoriously conservative when these forecasts were based on average experience. In the late 1920s L. I. Dublin, the chief actuary of the Metropolitan Life Insurance Company, put a cap of 64.75 years on life expectancy for both men and women. In 1936 he collaborated with the leading mathematical demographer of the first half of the twentieth century to publish a revised upper limit of 69.93 years.[4] More recently, a leading gerontologist set an upper limit on life (excluding some major breakthrough in molecular biology) of 85 plus or minus 7 years.[5] Generally speaking, these caps tend to be in the range of 5 to 10 years beyond the observed life expectancy at the time the forecasts were published.[6]

The accelerating decline in the prevalence of chronic diseases during the course of the twentieth century supports the proposition that increases in life expectancy during the twenty-first century will be fairly large. At the beginning of the twentieth century the burden of chronic diseases among elderly Americans was not only more severe but began more than 10 years earlier in the life cycle than it does today. Moreover, the number of comorbidities at each age between 50 and 70 is well below levels that prevailed a century ago. This is, according to one study, equivalent to pushing back old age, since an increase of one unit in a comorbidity index is the equivalent of being a decade older. Studies of changes in functional limitations among persons who have reached age 65 since the early 1980s indicate that such limitations declined at an accelerating rate during the balance of the 1980s and the 1990s.[7]

Dora Costa has found that favorable changes in body size, particularly the decline in the waist-to-hip ratio (a measure of abdominal fat), explained close to half of the decline in mortality rates above age 65 during the course of the twentieth century.[8] Taking account of the characteristics of men of military age in 1988, she predicts that the annual decline in male mortality rates after age 65 will be nearly twice as high between 1988 and 2022 as it was between 1914 and 1988. Overall, the work on trends in chronic diseases and on frame sizes tends to support forecasts of continued linear trends in the extension of longevity during the twenty-first century.

One factor arguing in support of the optimists' projections is the increasing span of years that individuals have free of chronic conditions. For those who reached age 65 during the first decade of the twentieth century, the average age of onset of chronic disabilities was about 51. By the 1990s, however, the average age of onset of chronic conditions was more than 10 years later. Moreover, these disabilities are now generally milder, and many effective interventions to reduce the impact of chronic conditions are available.[9] The outlook for new and more effective technologies to deal with chronic disabilities through the marriage of biology and microchip technology is very promising. Indeed, some devices that combine living cells and electronics to replace failed organs are already at the stage of human trials.[10] Somewhat further off, but even more promising, are advances in genetic engineering that will produce cures for what are now untreatable diseases.[11]

Appendix

If the relative risks of mortality in Figure 2.4 are standard-ized on the French crude death rate of c. 1785, one obtains the time series of crude death rates (per thousand) shown in Table A1.

Table IV in Waaler (1984) contains relative mortality rates for Norwegian males aged 50 to 64, averaged over height intervals of 10 cm and weight intervals of 10 kg. Attempts to fit iso-risk curves to these averages produced unsatisfactory results. Because at that time we did not have access to the data from which these averages were derived, it seemed reasonable to "fill in" the table by polynomial interpolation and use the generated data to estimate the risk–height–weight relationship.[1]

The interpolation was done in two steps. The first step consisted of taking the relative mortality rates given in the table and us-ing standard least-squares regressions to fit polynomials in weight to each column of risk values (corresponding to given levels of height) and polynomials in height to each row (corresponding to given levels of weight). These polynomials, which were each of the maximum order permitted by the number of entries in the

Table A1 Relative Risks of Mortality

	Death Rates per Thousand	
Date (approx.)	Estimated from Figure 2.4	From Registrations or Samples
1705	40	–
1785	36	36
1867	24	25
1967	19	11

corresponding row or column, were then used to generate values across each row and down each column of the table in intervals of whole centimeters and kilograms. This step generated 700 data points.

To further increase the available data, the rows and columns generated in the first step were used as the data for the second round of polynomial interpolations. The methodology was the same as that used in the first round and brought the total number of data points to 70,000.

The 70,000 triplets of height, weight, and relative mortality rates were then used to estimate a cubic response surface or production function of risk for inputs of height and weight:

$$R = F(H, W) + \varepsilon \tag{1}$$

where

$$F(H, W) = \sum_{0 \le i+k \le 3} \beta_{ik} H^i W^k \tag{2}$$

R = relative mortality risk, H = height in meters, W = weight in kilograms, β_{ik} is the coefficient on $H^i W^k$, and ε is a random disturbance term. Polynomials of degree 4 and higher improved the fit only marginally at considerable computational expense, yielding surfaces whose contour plots were all almost identical to the cubic's. The quadratic form was rejected because of the severe restrictions it imposes: it has a straight minimum-risk curve, which in general forces the estimated minimum-risk curve to lie to the right of the true curve.

The minimum-risk curve is defined as the locus of (H, W) pairs such that W minimizes the relative mortality risk, given H. Hence, given an estimated response surface $\hat{R} = \hat{F}(H, W)$, its equation is derived as

$$O = \frac{\partial \hat{R}}{\partial W} = \frac{\partial}{\partial W} \hat{F}(H, W) \tag{3}$$

from which it is easily seen that a quadratic $\hat{F}$ would necessarily have a linear minimum-risk curve.

Finally, an iso-risk curve on which $\hat{R} = r$ is simply

$$\hat{F}(H, W) - r = 0 \tag{4}$$

while an iso-BMI curve for BMI $= b$ is by definition

$$W - bH^2 = 0. \tag{5}$$

The frontispiece shows the mortality risk surface that corresponds to Figure 2.4 in the text. Table A2 gives the relative mortality risks by weight and height. Table A3 gives the relative mortality risks by BMI and height, and also shows the optimal BMI and the corresponding risk for each height.

Table A2 Relative Mortality Risk Table for Norwegian Males Aged 50–64, by Weight (kg) and Height (m)

m kg	40	41	42	43	44	45	46	47	48	49	50
1.55	2.18	2.10	2.02	1.95	1.88	1.81	1.75	1.70	1.65	1.60	1.56
1.56	2.22	2.14	2.06	1.98	1.91	1.84	1.78	1.72	1.66	1.61	1.57
1.57	2.27	2.18	2.09	2.01	1.94	1.86	1.80	1.74	1.68	1.63	1.58
1.58	2.31	2.22	2.13	2.04	1.97	1.89	1.82	1.76	1.70	1.64	1.59
1.59	2.35	2.26	2.16	2.08	2.00	1.92	1.85	1.78	1.72	1.66	1.60
1.60	2.40	2.30	2.20	2.11	2.03	1.95	1.87	1.80	1.74	1.67	1.62
1.61	2.44	2.34	2.24	2.15	2.06	1.98	1.90	1.83	1.76	1.69	1.63
1.62	2.49	2.38	2.28	2.18	2.09	2.01	1.93	1.85	1.78	1.71	1.65
1.63	2.53	2.42	2.32	2.22	2.13	2.04	1.96	1.88	1.80	1.73	1.66
1.64	2.58	2.47	2.36	2.26	2.16	2.07	1.98	1.90	1.82	1.75	1.68
1.65	2.63	2.51	2.40	2.30	2.20	2.10	2.01	1.93	1.85	1.77	1.70
1.66	2.67	2.56	2.44	2.34	2.23	2.14	2.04	1.96	1.87	1.80	1.72
1.67	2.72	2.60	2.49	2.38	2.27	2.17	2.08	1.99	1.90	1.82	1.74
1.68	2.77	2.65	2.53	2.42	2.31	2.21	2.11	2.01	1.93	1.84	1.76
1.69	2.82	2.69	2.57	2.46	2.35	2.24	2.14	2.04	1.95	1.87	1.79
1.70	2.87	2.74	2.61	2.50	2.38	2.28	2.17	2.08	1.98	1.89	1.81
1.71	2.92	2.78	2.66	2.54	2.42	2.31	2.21	2.11	2.01	1.92	1.83
1.72	2.97	2.83	2.70	2.58	2.46	2.35	2.24	2.14	2.04	1.95	1.86
1.73	3.02	2.88	2.75	2.62	2.50	2.39	2.27	2.17	2.07	1.97	1.88
1.74	3.06	2.93	2.79	2.66	2.54	2.42	2.31	2.20	2.10	2.00	1.91
1.75	3.11	2.97	2.84	2.71	2.58	2.46	2.34	2.23	2.13	2.03	1.93
1.76	3.16	3.02	2.88	2.75	2.62	2.50	2.38	2.27	2.16	2.06	1.96
1.77	3.21	3.07	2.93	2.79	2.66	2.54	2.42	2.30	2.19	2.09	1.99
1.78	3.26	3.12	2.97	2.83	2.70	2.57	2.45	2.34	2.22	2.12	2.02
1.79	3.31	3.16	3.02	2.88	2.74	2.61	2.49	2.37	2.26	2.15	2.04
1.80	3.36	3.21	3.06	2.92	2.78	2.65	2.53	2.40	2.29	2.18	2.07
1.81	3.41	3.26	3.11	2.96	2.82	2.69	2.56	2.44	2.32	2.21	2.10
1.82	3.46	3.31	3.15	3.01	2.86	2.73	2.60	2.47	2.35	2.24	2.13
1.83	3.51	3.35	3.20	3.05	2.91	2.77	2.63	2.51	2.39	2.27	2.16
1.84	3.56	3.40	3.24	3.09	2.95	2.81	2.67	2.54	2.42	2.30	2.19
1.85	3.61	3.45	3.29	3.13	2.99	2.84	2.71	2.58	2.45	2.33	2.22
1.86	3.66	3.49	3.33	3.18	3.03	2.88	2.75	2.61	2.48	2.36	2.25
1.87	3.71	3.54	3.38	3.22	3.07	2.92	2.78	2.65	2.52	2.39	2.28
1.88	3.76	3.58	3.42	3.26	3.11	2.96	2.82	2.68	2.55	2.43	2.30
1.89	3.80	3.63	3.46	3.30	3.15	3.00	2.85	2.72	2.58	2.46	2.33
1.90	3.85	3.67	3.51	3.34	3.19	3.04	2.89	2.75	2.62	2.49	2.36
1.91	3.90	3.72	3.55	3.38	3.23	3.07	2.93	2.78	2.65	2.52	2.39
1.92	3.94	3.76	3.59	3.42	3.26	3.11	2.96	2.82	2.68	2.55	2.42
1.93	3.99	3.81	3.63	3.46	3.30	3.15	3.00	2.85	2.71	2.58	2.45
1.94	4.03	3.85	3.67	3.50	3.34	3.18	3.03	2.89	2.75	2.61	2.48
1.95	4.08	3.89	3.71	3.54	3.38	3.22	3.07	2.92	2.78	2.64	2.51

m kg	51	52	53	54	55	56	57	58	59	60	61
1.55	1.52	1.48	1.45	1.42	1.40	1.38	1.36	1.35	1.34	1.33	1.33
1.56	1.52	1.49	1.45	1.42	1.39	1.37	1.35	1.33	1.32	1.31	1.30
1.57	1.53	1.49	1.45	1.42	1.39	1.36	1.34	1.32	1.31	1.29	1.28
1.58	1.54	1.50	1.46	1.42	1.39	1.36	1.33	1.31	1.29	1.28	1.27
1.59	1.55	1.50	1.46	1.42	1.39	1.36	1.33	1.30	1.28	1.26	1.25
1.60	1.56	1.51	1.47	1.43	1.39	1.35	1.32	1.30	1.27	1.25	1.24
1.61	1.57	1.52	1.47	1.43	1.39	1.35	1.32	1.29	1.26	1.24	1.22
1.62	1.59	1.53	1.48	1.44	1.39	1.35	1.32	1.29	1.26	1.23	1.21
1.63	1.60	1.55	1.49	1.44	1.40	1.35	1.32	1.28	1.25	1.22	1.20
1.64	1.62	1.56	1.50	1.45	1.40	1.36	1.32	1.28	1.25	1.22	1.19
1.65	1.63	1.57	1.51	1.46	1.41	1.36	1.32	1.28	1.24	1.21	1.18
1.66	1.65	1.59	1.53	1.47	1.42	1.37	1.32	1.28	1.24	1.21	1.18
1.67	1.67	1.60	1.54	1.48	1.42	1.37	1.33	1.28	1.24	1.20	1.17
1.68	1.69	1.62	1.55	1.49	1.43	1.38	1.33	1.28	1.24	1.20	1.17
1.69	1.71	1.64	1.57	1.50	1.44	1.39	1.34	1.29	1.24	1.20	1.17
1.70	1.73	1.65	1.58	1.52	1.46	1.40	1.34	1.29	1.25	1.20	1.16
1.71	1.75	1.67	1.60	1.53	1.47	1.41	1.35	1.30	1.25	1.21	1.16
1.72	1.77	1.69	1.62	1.55	1.48	1.42	1.36	1.31	1.25	1.21	1.16
1.73	1.80	1.71	1.64	1.56	1.50	1.43	1.37	1.31	1.26	1.21	1.17
1.74	1.82	1.74	1.66	1.58	1.51	1.44	1.38	1.32	1.27	1.22	1.17
1.75	1.84	1.76	1.68	1.60	1.53	1.46	1.39	1.33	1.28	1.22	1.17
1.76	1.87	1.78	1.70	1.62	1.54	1.47	1.40	1.34	1.28	1.23	1.18
1.77	1.89	1.80	1.72	1.64	1.56	1.49	1.42	1.35	1.29	1.24	1.19
1.78	1.92	1.83	1.74	1.66	1.58	1.50	1.43	1.37	1.30	1.25	1.19
1.79	1.94	1.85	1.76	1.68	1.59	1.52	1.45	1.38	1.31	1.26	1.20
1.80	1.97	1.87	1.78	1.70	1.61	1.54	1.46	1.39	1.33	1.27	1.21
1.81	2.00	1.90	1.81	1.72	1.63	1.55	1.48	1.41	1.34	1.28	1.22
1.82	2.02	1.92	1.83	1.74	1.65	1.57	1.49	1.42	1.35	1.29	1.23
1.83	2.05	1.95	1.85	1.76	1.67	1.59	1.51	1.44	1.37	1.30	1.24
1.84	2.08	1.98	1.88	1.78	1.69	1.61	1.53	1.45	1.38	1.31	1.25
1.85	2.11	2.00	1.90	1.80	1.71	1.63	1.55	1.47	1.40	1.33	1.26
1.86	2.13	2.03	1.92	1.83	1.74	1.65	1.56	1.49	1.41	1.34	1.27
1.87	2.16	2.05	1.95	1.85	1.76	1.67	1.58	1.50	1.43	1.35	1.29
1.88	2.19	2.08	1.97	1.87	1.78	1.69	1.60	1.52	1.44	1.37	1.30
1.89	2.22	2.11	2.00	1.90	1.80	1.71	1.62	1.54	1.46	1.38	1.31
1.90	2.25	2.13	2.02	1.92	1.82	1.73	1.64	1.56	1.48	1.40	1.33
1.91	2.27	2.16	2.05	1.94	1.84	1.75	1.66	1.57	1.49	1.42	1.34
1.92	2.30	2.19	2.07	1.97	1.87	1.77	1.68	1.59	1.51	1.43	1.36
1.93	2.33	2.21	2.10	1.99	1.89	1.79	1.70	1.61	1.53	1.45	1.37
1.94	2.36	2.24	2.12	2.02	1.91	1.81	1.72	1.63	1.55	1.47	1.39
1.95	2.38	2.26	2.15	2.04	1.93	1.83	1.74	1.65	1.56	1.48	1.41

(continued)

Table A2 *(continued)*

m kg	62	63	64	65	66	67	68	69	70	71	72
1.55	1.32	1.33	1.33	1.34	1.35	1.36	1.37	1.39	1.41	1.43	1.46
1.56	1.30	1.30	1.30	1.31	1.31	1.32	1.34	1.35	1.37	1.39	1.41
1.57	1.28	1.28	1.27	1.28	1.28	1.29	1.30	1.31	1.33	1.34	1.36
1.58	1.26	1.25	1.25	1.25	1.25	1.26	1.26	1.27	1.29	1.30	1.32
1.59	1.24	1.23	1.23	1.22	1.22	1.23	1.23	1.24	1.25	1.26	1.28
1.60	1.22	1.21	1.20	1.20	1.20	1.20	1.20	1.21	1.21	1.22	1.24
1.61	1.21	1.19	1.18	1.18	1.17	1.17	1.17	1.17	1.18	1.19	1.20
1.62	1.19	1.18	1.16	1.15	1.15	1.14	1.14	1.14	1.15	1.15	1.16
1.63	1.18	1.16	1.15	1.13	1.13	1.12	1.12	1.12	1.12	1.12	1.13
1.64	1.17	1.15	1.13	1.12	1.11	1.10	1.09	1.09	1.09	1.09	1.10
1.65	1.16	1.14	1.12	1.10	1.09	1.08	1.07	1.07	1.06	1.06	1.07
1.66	1.15	1.12	1.10	1.09	1.07	1.06	1.05	1.04	1.04	1.04	1.04
1.67	1.14	1.12	1.09	1.07	1.06	1.04	1.03	1.02	1.02	1.01	1.01
1.68	1.14	1.11	1.08	1.06	1.04	1.03	1.01	1.00	0.99	0.99	0.99
1.69	1.13	1.10	1.07	1.05	1.03	1.01	1.00	0.98	0.98	0.97	0.96
1.70	1.13	1.10	1.07	1.04	1.02	1.00	0.98	0.97	0.96	0.95	0.94
1.71	1.13	1.09	1.06	1.03	1.01	0.99	0.97	0.95	0.94	0.93	0.92
1.72	1.13	1.09	1.06	1.03	1.00	0.98	0.96	0.94	0.93	0.91	0.90
1.73	1.13	1.09	1.05	1.02	0.99	0.97	0.95	0.93	0.91	0.90	0.89
1.74	1.13	1.09	1.05	1.02	0.99	0.96	0.94	0.92	0.90	0.89	0.87
1.75	1.13	1.09	1.05	1.01	0.98	0.95	0.93	0.91	0.89	0.87	0.86
1.76	1.13	1.09	1.05	1.01	0.98	0.95	0.92	0.90	0.88	0.86	0.85
1.77	1.14	1.09	1.05	1.01	0.98	0.95	0.92	0.89	0.87	0.85	0.84
1.78	1.14	1.09	1.05	1.01	0.98	0.94	0.91	0.89	0.86	0.84	0.83
1.79	1.15	1.10	1.05	1.01	0.98	0.94	0.91	0.88	0.86	0.84	0.82
1.80	1.15	1.10	1.06	1.02	0.98	0.94	0.91	0.88	0.85	0.83	0.81
1.81	1.16	1.11	1.06	1.02	0.98	0.94	0.91	0.88	0.85	0.83	0.81
1.82	1.17	1.12	1.07	1.02	0.98	0.94	0.91	0.88	0.85	0.82	0.80
1.83	1.18	1.13	1.08	1.03	0.99	0.95	0.91	0.88	0.85	0.82	0.80
1.84	1.19	1.13	1.08	1.03	0.99	0.95	0.91	0.88	0.85	0.82	0.80
1.85	1.20	1.14	1.09	1.04	1.00	0.95	0.92	0.88	0.85	0.82	0.79
1.86	1.21	1.15	1.10	1.05	1.00	0.96	0.92	0.88	0.85	0.82	0.79
1.87	1.22	1.16	1.11	1.06	1.01	0.97	0.92	0.89	0.85	0.82	0.80
1.88	1.24	1.18	1.12	1.07	1.02	0.97	0.93	0.89	0.86	0.83	0.80
1.89	1.25	1.19	1.13	1.08	1.03	0.98	0.94	0.90	0.86	0.83	0.80
1.90	1.26	1.20	1.14	1.09	1.03	0.99	0.94	0.90	0.87	0.83	0.80
1.91	1.28	1.21	1.15	1.10	1.04	1.00	0.95	0.91	0.87	0.84	0.81
1.92	1.29	1.23	1.16	1.11	1.05	1.01	0.96	0.92	0.88	0.85	0.81
1.93	1.30	1.24	1.18	1.12	1.07	1.02	0.97	0.93	0.89	0.85	0.82
1.94	1.32	1.25	1.19	1.13	1.08	1.03	0.98	0.94	0.90	0.86	0.83
1.95	1.33	1.27	1.20	1.14	1.09	1.04	0.99	0.94	0.90	0.87	0.83

m kg	73	74	75	76	77	78	79	80	81	82	83
1.55	1.48	1.51	1.54	1.57	1.60	1.64	1.67	1.71	1.75	1.78	1.82
1.56	1.43	1.46	1.48	1.51	1.54	1.57	1.61	1.64	1.68	1.72	1.75
1.57	1.38	1.41	1.43	1.46	1.49	1.52	1.55	1.58	1.61	1.65	1.69
1.58	1.34	1.36	1.38	1.41	1.43	1.46	1.49	1.52	1.55	1.59	1.62
1.59	1.29	1.31	1.33	1.36	1.38	1.41	1.43	1.46	1.49	1.53	1.56
1.60	1.25	1.27	1.29	1.31	1.33	1.35	1.38	1.41	1.44	1.47	1.50
1.61	1.21	1.23	1.24	1.26	1.28	1.31	1.33	1.35	1.38	1.41	1.44
1.62	1.17	1.19	1.20	1.22	1.24	1.26	1.28	1.30	1.33	1.36	1.38
1.63	1.14	1.15	1.16	1.18	1.19	1.21	1.23	1.26	1.28	1.31	1.33
1.64	1.10	1.11	1.13	1.14	1.15	1.17	1.19	1.21	1.23	1.26	1.28
1.65	1.07	1.08	1.09	1.10	1.11	1.13	1.15	1.17	1.19	1.21	1.23
1.66	1.04	1.05	1.06	1.07	1.08	1.09	1.11	1.12	1.14	1.16	1.19
1.67	1.01	1.02	1.02	1.03	1.04	1.06	1.07	1.09	1.10	1.12	1.14
1.68	0.99	0.99	0.99	1.00	1.01	1.02	1.03	1.05	1.06	1.08	1.10
1.69	0.96	0.96	0.97	0.97	0.98	0.99	1.00	1.01	1.03	1.04	1.06
1.70	0.94	0.94	0.94	0.94	0.95	0.96	0.97	0.98	0.99	1.01	1.02
1.71	0.92	0.92	0.92	0.92	0.92	0.93	0.94	0.95	0.96	0.97	0.99
1.72	0.90	0.89	0.89	0.89	0.90	0.90	0.91	0.92	0.93	0.94	0.96
1.73	0.88	0.88	0.87	0.87	0.87	0.88	0.88	0.89	0.90	0.91	0.92
1.74	0.86	0.86	0.85	0.85	0.85	0.85	0.86	0.86	0.87	0.88	0.90
1.75	0.85	0.84	0.83	0.83	0.83	0.83	0.84	0.84	0.85	0.86	0.87
1.76	0.83	0.83	0.82	0.81	0.81	0.81	0.81	0.82	0.82	0.83	0.84
1.77	0.82	0.81	0.80	0.80	0.79	0.79	0.79	0.80	0.80	0.81	0.82
1.78	0.81	0.80	0.79	0.78	0.78	0.78	0.78	0.78	0.78	0.79	0.80
1.79	0.80	0.79	0.78	0.77	0.77	0.76	0.76	0.76	0.77	0.77	0.78
1.80	0.79	0.78	0.77	0.76	0.75	0.75	0.75	0.75	0.75	0.75	0.76
1.81	0.79	0.77	0.76	0.75	0.74	0.74	0.73	0.73	0.73	0.74	0.74
1.82	0.78	0.77	0.75	0.74	0.73	0.73	0.72	0.72	0.72	0.72	0.73
1.83	0.78	0.76	0.74	0.73	0.72	0.72	0.71	0.71	0.71	0.71	0.72
1.84	0.77	0.76	0.74	0.73	0.72	0.71	0.70	0.70	0.70	0.70	0.70
1.85	0.77	0.75	0.74	0.72	0.71	0.70	0.70	0.69	0.69	0.69	0.69
1.86	0.77	0.75	0.73	0.72	0.71	0.70	0.69	0.69	0.68	0.68	0.69
1.87	0.77	0.75	0.73	0.72	0.70	0.69	0.69	0.68	0.68	0.68	0.68
1.88	0.77	0.75	0.73	0.71	0.70	0.69	0.68	0.68	0.67	0.67	0.67
1.89	0.77	0.75	0.73	0.71	0.70	0.69	0.68	0.67	0.67	0.67	0.67
1.90	0.78	0.75	0.73	0.72	0.70	0.69	0.68	0.67	0.67	0.67	0.67
1.91	0.78	0.76	0.74	0.72	0.70	0.69	0.68	0.67	0.67	0.66	0.66
1.92	0.79	0.76	0.74	0.72	0.70	0.69	0.68	0.67	0.67	0.66	0.66
1.93	0.79	0.77	0.74	0.72	0.71	0.69	0.68	0.67	0.67	0.67	0.66
1.94	0.80	0.77	0.75	0.73	0.71	0.70	0.69	0.68	0.67	0.67	0.67
1.95	0.80	0.78	0.75	0.73	0.72	0.70	0.69	0.68	0.68	0.67	0.67

(continued)

Table A2 *(continued)*

m kg	84	85	86	87	88	89	90	91	92	93	94
1.55	1.87	1.91	1.95	1.99	2.04	2.08	2.13	2.17	2.22	2.26	2.31
1.56	1.79	1.83	1.87	1.92	1.96	2.00	2.05	2.09	2.13	2.18	2.22
1.57	1.72	1.76	1.80	1.84	1.88	1.92	1.97	2.01	2.05	2.09	2.14
1.58	1.66	1.69	1.73	1.77	1.81	1.85	1.89	1.93	1.97	2.01	2.05
1.59	1.59	1.63	1.66	1.70	1.74	1.78	1.81	1.85	1.89	1.93	1.97
1.60	1.53	1.56	1.60	1.63	1.67	1.71	1.74	1.78	1.82	1.86	1.90
1.61	1.47	1.50	1.54	1.57	1.60	1.64	1.67	1.71	1.75	1.79	1.82
1.62	1.41	1.44	1.48	1.51	1.54	1.57	1.61	1.64	1.68	1.72	1.75
1.63	1.36	1.39	1.42	1.45	1.48	1.51	1.55	1.58	1.61	1.65	1.68
1.64	1.31	1.33	1.36	1.39	1.42	1.45	1.49	1.52	1.55	1.59	1.62
1.65	1.26	1.28	1.31	1.34	1.37	1.40	1.43	1.46	1.49	1.52	1.56
1.66	1.21	1.23	1.26	1.29	1.31	1.34	1.37	1.40	1.43	1.47	1.50
1.67	1.16	1.19	1.21	1.24	1.26	1.29	1.32	1.35	1.38	1.41	1.44
1.68	1.12	1.14	1.17	1.19	1.22	1.24	1.27	1.30	1.33	1.36	1.39
1.69	1.08	1.10	1.12	1.15	1.17	1.20	1.22	1.25	1.28	1.31	1.33
1.70	1.04	1.06	1.08	1.10	1.13	1.15	1.18	1.20	1.23	1.26	1.29
1.71	1.01	1.02	1.04	1.07	1.09	1.11	1.13	1.16	1.19	1.21	1.24
1.72	0.97	0.99	1.01	1.03	1.05	1.07	1.09	1.12	1.14	1.17	1.20
1.73	0.94	0.96	0.97	0.99	1.01	1.03	1.06	1.08	1.10	1.13	1.15
1.74	0.91	0.92	0.94	0.96	0.98	1.00	1.02	1.04	1.07	1.09	1.12
1.75	0.88	0.90	0.91	0.93	0.95	0.97	0.99	1.01	1.03	1.05	1.08
1.76	0.85	0.87	0.88	0.90	0.92	0.94	0.95	0.98	1.00	1.02	1.04
1.77	0.83	0.84	0.86	0.87	0.89	0.91	0.93	0.95	0.97	0.99	1.01
1.78	0.81	0.82	0.83	0.85	0.86	0.88	0.90	0.92	0.94	0.96	0.98
1.79	0.79	0.80	0.81	0.82	0.84	0.86	0.87	0.89	0.91	0.93	0.96
1.80	0.77	0.78	0.79	0.80	0.82	0.83	0.85	0.87	0.89	0.91	0.93
1.81	0.75	0.76	0.77	0.78	0.80	0.81	0.83	0.85	0.87	0.89	0.91
1.82	0.74	0.74	0.75	0.77	0.78	0.79	0.81	0.83	0.85	0.87	0.89
1.83	0.72	0.73	0.74	0.75	0.76	0.78	0.79	0.81	0.83	0.85	0.87
1.84	0.71	0.72	0.73	0.74	0.75	0.76	0.78	0.79	0.81	0.83	0.85
1.85	0.70	0.71	0.71	0.72	0.74	0.75	0.76	0.78	0.80	0.82	0.84
1.86	0.69	0.70	0.70	0.71	0.72	0.74	0.75	0.77	0.79	0.80	0.82
1.87	0.68	0.69	0.70	0.70	0.72	0.73	0.74	0.76	0.78	0.79	0.81
1.88	0.68	0.68	0.69	0.70	0.71	0.72	0.73	0.75	0.77	0.79	0.80
1.89	0.67	0.68	0.68	0.69	0.70	0.71	0.73	0.74	0.76	0.78	0.80
1.90	0.67	0.67	0.68	0.69	0.70	0.71	0.72	0.74	0.76	0.77	0.79
1.91	0.67	0.67	0.68	0.68	0.69	0.71	0.72	0.74	0.75	0.77	0.79
1.92	0.67	0.67	0.68	0.68	0.69	0.71	0.72	0.73	0.75	0.77	0.79
1.93	0.67	0.67	0.68	0.68	0.69	0.71	0.72	0.73	0.75	0.77	0.79
1.94	0.67	0.67	0.68	0.69	0.69	0.71	0.72	0.73	0.75	0.77	0.79
1.95	0.67	0.67	0.68	0.69	0.70	0.71	0.72	0.74	0.75	0.77	0.79

m kg	95	96	97	98	99	100	101	102	103	104	105
1.55	2.36	2.40	2.45	2.49	2.54	2.58	2.62	2.67	2.71	2.75	2.79
1.56	2.27	2.31	2.35	2.40	2.44	2.48	2.53	2.57	2.61	2.65	2.69
1.57	2.18	2.22	2.26	2.31	2.35	2.39	2.43	2.47	2.51	2.55	2.59
1.58	2.09	2.14	2.18	2.22	2.26	2.30	2.34	2.38	2.42	2.46	2.49
1.59	2.01	2.05	2.09	2.13	2.17	2.21	2.25	2.29	2.33	2.36	2.40
1.60	1.94	1.97	2.01	2.05	2.09	2.13	2.17	2.20	2.24	2.28	2.31
1.61	1.86	1.90	1.94	1.97	2.01	2.05	2.08	2.12	2.16	2.19	2.23
1.62	1.79	1.83	1.86	1.90	1.93	1.97	2.01	2.04	2.08	2.11	2.14
1.63	1.72	1.76	1.79	1.83	1.86	1.90	1.93	1.97	2.00	2.03	2.07
1.64	1.65	1.69	1.72	1.76	1.79	1.83	1.86	1.89	1.93	1.96	1.99
1.65	1.59	1.62	1.66	1.69	1.72	1.76	1.79	1.82	1.86	1.89	1.92
1.66	1.53	1.56	1.59	1.63	1.66	1.69	1.72	1.76	1.79	1.82	1.85
1.67	1.47	1.50	1.53	1.57	1.60	1.63	1.66	1.69	1.72	1.75	1.78
1.68	1.42	1.45	1.48	1.51	1.54	1.57	1.60	1.63	1.66	1.69	1.72
1.69	1.36	1.39	1.42	1.45	1.48	1.51	1.54	1.57	1.60	1.63	1.66
1.70	1.31	1.34	1.37	1.40	1.43	1.46	1.49	1.52	1.55	1.58	1.61
1.71	1.27	1.30	1.32	1.35	1.38	1.41	1.44	1.47	1.50	1.52	1.55
1.72	1.22	1.25	1.28	1.31	1.33	1.36	1.39	1.42	1.45	1.47	1.50
1.73	1.18	1.21	1.23	1.26	1.29	1.32	1.34	1.37	1.40	1.43	1.45
1.74	1.14	1.17	1.19	1.22	1.25	1.27	1.30	1.33	1.36	1.38	1.41
1.75	1.10	1.13	1.15	1.18	1.21	1.23	1.26	1.29	1.32	1.34	1.37
1.76	1.07	1.09	1.12	1.14	1.17	1.20	1.22	1.25	1.28	1.30	1.33
1.77	1.04	1.06	1.09	1.11	1.14	1.16	1.19	1.22	1.24	1.27	1.29
1.78	1.01	1.03	1.05	1.08	1.10	1.13	1.16	1.18	1.21	1.23	1.26
1.79	0.98	1.00	1.03	1.05	1.08	1.10	1.13	1.15	1.18	1.20	1.23
1.80	0.95	0.98	1.00	1.02	1.05	1.07	1.10	1.12	1.15	1.18	1.20
1.81	0.93	0.95	0.98	1.00	1.02	1.05	1.07	1.10	1.13	1.15	1.18
1.82	0.91	0.93	0.95	0.98	1.00	1.03	1.05	1.08	1.10	1.13	1.15
1.83	0.89	0.91	0.93	0.96	0.98	1.01	1.03	1.06	1.08	1.11	1.13
1.84	0.87	0.89	0.92	0.94	0.96	0.99	1.01	1.04	1.07	1.09	1.12
1.85	0.86	0.88	0.90	0.93	0.95	0.97	1.00	1.02	1.05	1.08	1.10
1.86	0.84	0.87	0.89	0.91	0.94	0.96	0.99	1.01	1.04	1.06	1.09
1.87	0.83	0.86	0.88	0.90	0.93	0.95	0.97	1.00	1.03	1.05	1.08
1.88	0.82	0.85	0.87	0.89	0.92	0.94	0.97	0.99	1.02	1.04	1.07
1.89	0.82	0.84	0.86	0.89	0.91	0.93	0.96	0.99	1.01	1.04	1.07
1.90	0.81	0.83	0.86	0.88	0.90	0.93	0.96	0.98	1.01	1.04	1.06
1.91	0.81	0.83	0.85	0.88	0.90	0.93	0.95	0.98	1.01	1.03	1.06
1.92	0.81	0.83	0.85	0.88	0.90	0.93	0.95	0.98	1.01	1.03	1.06
1.93	0.81	0.83	0.85	0.88	0.90	0.93	0.95	0.98	1.01	1.04	1.07
1.94	0.81	0.83	0.86	0.88	0.91	0.93	0.96	0.99	1.01	1.04	1.07
1.95	0.81	0.84	0.86	0.88	0.91	0.94	0.96	0.99	1.02	1.05	1.08

(continued)

Table A2 *(continued)*

m kg	106	107	108	109	110
1.55	2.83	2.87	2.90	2.94	2.97
1.56	2.72	2.76	2.80	2.83	2.87
1.57	2.62	2.66	2.70	2.73	2.76
1.58	2.53	2.56	2.60	2.63	2.66
1.59	2.44	2.47	2.50	2.53	2.56
1.60	2.35	2.38	2.41	2.44	2.47
1.61	2.26	2.29	2.32	2.35	2.38
1.62	2.18	2.21	2.24	2.27	2.30
1.63	2.10	2.13	2.16	2.19	2.22
1.64	2.02	2.05	2.08	2.11	2.14
1.65	1.95	1.98	2.01	2.03	2.06
1.66	1.88	1.91	1.94	1.96	1.99
1.67	1.81	1.84	1.87	1.90	1.92
1.68	1.75	1.78	1.81	1.83	1.86
1.69	1.69	1.72	1.74	1.77	1.80
1.70	1.63	1.66	1.69	1.71	1.74
1.71	1.58	1.61	1.63	1.66	1.68
1.72	1.53	1.56	1.58	1.61	1.63
1.73	1.48	1.51	1.53	1.56	1.58
1.74	1.44	1.46	1.49	1.51	1.54
1.75	1.39	1.42	1.45	1.47	1.49
1.76	1.36	1.38	1.41	1.43	1.45
1.77	1.32	1.34	1.37	1.39	1.42
1.78	1.29	1.31	1.34	1.36	1.38
1.79	1.26	1.28	1.31	1.33	1.35
1.80	1.23	1.25	1.28	1.30	1.33
1.81	1.20	1.23	1.25	1.28	1.30
1.82	1.18	1.20	1.23	1.25	1.28
1.83	1.16	1.19	1.21	1.24	1.26
1.84	1.14	1.17	1.19	1.22	1.24
1.85	1.13	1.15	1.18	1.20	1.23
1.86	1.12	1.14	1.17	1.19	1.22
1.87	1.11	1.13	1.16	1.18	1.21
1.88	1.10	1.12	1.15	1.18	1.20
1.89	1.09	1.12	1.15	1.17	1.20
1.90	1.09	1.12	1.14	1.17	1.20
1.91	1.09	1.12	1.15	1.17	1.20
1.92	1.09	1.12	1.15	1.18	1.20
1.93	1.10	1.12	1.15	1.18	1.21
1.94	1.10	1.13	1.16	1.19	1.22
1.95	1.11	1.14	1.17	1.20	1.23

Table A3 Relative Mortality Risk Table for Norwegian Males Aged 50–64, by BMI and Height, Also Showing the Optimal BMI and Minimum Risk at Each Height

m BMI	17	18	19	20	21	22	23	24	25	26
1.55	2.11	1.93	1.77	1.64	1.54	1.46	1.39	1.35	1.33	1.33
1.56	2.11	1.92	1.76	1.63	1.52	1.43	1.37	1.33	1.31	1.30
1.57	2.10	1.91	1.75	1.61	1.50	1.41	1.35	1.30	1.28	1.27
1.58	2.09	1.90	1.73	1.59	1.48	1.39	1.32	1.28	1.26	1.25
1.59	2.08	1.88	1.71	1.57	1.46	1.37	1.30	1.25	1.23	1.22
1.60	2.07	1.87	1.70	1.55	1.44	1.34	1.28	1.23	1.20	1.20
1.61	2.05	1.85	1.68	1.53	1.41	1.32	1.25	1.20	1.18	1.17
1.62	2.04	1.83	1.66	1.51	1.39	1.29	1.22	1.18	1.15	1.14
1.63	2.02	1.81	1.63	1.48	1.36	1.27	1.20	1.15	1.12	1.12
1.64	2.01	1.79	1.61	1.46	1.34	1.24	1.17	1.12	1.10	1.09
1.65	1.99	1.77	1.59	1.44	1.31	1.21	1.14	1.10	1.07	1.06
1.66	1.97	1.75	1.56	1.41	1.28	1.19	1.12	1.07	1.04	1.04
1.67	1.95	1.73	1.54	1.38	1.26	1.16	1.09	1.04	1.02	1.01
1.68	1.93	1.70	1.51	1.36	1.23	1.13	1.06	1.02	0.99	0.99
1.69	1.91	1.68	1.49	1.33	1.20	1.11	1.04	0.99	0.97	0.96
1.70	1.88	1.65	1.46	1.30	1.18	1.08	1.01	0.96	0.94	0.94
1.71	1.86	1.63	1.43	1.27	1.15	1.05	0.98	0.94	0.92	0.92
1.72	1.83	1.60	1.41	1.25	1.12	1.02	0.96	0.91	0.89	0.90
1.73	1.81	1.57	1.38	1.22	1.09	1.00	0.93	0.89	0.87	0.88
1.74	1.78	1.55	1.35	1.19	1.07	0.97	0.91	0.87	0.85	0.86
1.75	1.75	1.52	1.32	1.16	1.04	0.95	0.88	0.84	0.83	0.84
1.76	1.72	1.49	1.29	1.13	1.01	0.92	0.86	0.82	0.81	0.82
1.77	1.70	1.46	1.26	1.11	0.98	0.90	0.84	0.80	0.79	0.81
1.78	1.67	1.43	1.23	1.08	0.96	0.87	0.81	0.78	0.78	0.79
1.79	1.64	1.40	1.21	1.05	0.93	0.85	0.79	0.77	0.76	0.78
1.80	1.61	1.37	1.18	1.02	0.91	0.83	0.77	0.75	0.75	0.77
1.81	1.58	1.34	1.15	1.00	0.88	0.80	0.76	0.73	0.74	0.76
1.82	1.55	1.31	1.12	0.97	0.86	0.78	0.74	0.72	0.73	0.76
1.83	1.52	1.28	1.09	0.95	0.84	0.77	0.72	0.71	0.72	0.75
1.84	1.49	1.25	1.07	0.92	0.82	0.75	0.71	0.70	0.71	0.75
1.85	1.45	1.22	1.04	0.90	0.80	0.73	0.70	0.69	0.71	0.75
1.86	1.42	1.20	1.01	0.88	0.78	0.72	0.69	0.69	0.71	0.75
1.87	1.39	1.17	0.99	0.86	0.76	0.70	0.68	0.68	0.71	0.76
1.88	1.36	1.14	0.97	0.83	0.75	0.69	0.67	0.68	0.71	0.76
1.89	1.33	1.11	0.94	0.82	0.73	0.68	0.67	0.68	0.72	0.78
1.90	1.30	1.09	0.92	0.80	0.72	0.68	0.67	0.68	0.73	0.79
1.91	1.27	1.06	0.90	0.78	0.71	0.67	0.67	0.69	0.74	0.81
1.92	1.25	1.04	0.88	0.77	0.70	0.67	0.67	0.70	0.75	0.83
1.93	1.22	1.01	0.86	0.75	0.69	0.67	0.67	0.71	0.77	0.85
1.94	1.19	0.99	0.84	0.74	0.69	0.67	0.68	0.72	0.79	0.88
1.95	1.16	0.97	0.83	0.73	0.68	0.67	0.69	0.74	0.82	0.91

(continued)

Table A3 *(continued)*

m BMI	27	28	29	30	31	32	33	34	35	36
1.55	1.34	1.36	1.40	1.46	1.52	1.60	1.68	1.77	1.87	1.97
1.56	1.31	1.34	1.38	1.43	1.50	1.57	1.65	1.74	1.84	1.94
1.57	1.29	1.31	1.35	1.40	1.47	1.54	1.63	1.72	1.81	1.91
1.58	1.26	1.29	1.33	1.38	1.44	1.52	1.60	1.69	1.78	1.88
1.59	1.23	1.26	1.30	1.35	1.42	1.49	1.57	1.66	1.76	1.85
1.60	1.21	1.23	1.27	1.33	1.39	1.46	1.55	1.63	1.73	1.83
1.61	1.18	1.21	1.25	1.30	1.36	1.44	1.52	1.61	1.70	1.80
1.62	1.15	1.18	1.22	1.27	1.34	1.41	1.49	1.58	1.67	1.77
1.63	1.13	1.15	1.20	1.25	1.31	1.39	1.47	1.56	1.65	1.74
1.64	1.10	1.13	1.17	1.23	1.29	1.36	1.45	1.53	1.62	1.72
1.65	1.08	1.10	1.15	1.20	1.27	1.34	1.42	1.51	1.60	1.69
1.66	1.05	1.08	1.12	1.18	1.25	1.32	1.40	1.49	1.58	1.67
1.67	1.03	1.06	1.10	1.16	1.22	1.30	1.38	1.47	1.55	1.64
1.68	1.00	1.03	1.08	1.14	1.20	1.28	1.36	1.45	1.53	1.62
1.69	0.98	1.01	1.06	1.12	1.18	1.26	1.34	1.43	1.51	1.60
1.70	0.96	0.99	1.04	1.10	1.17	1.24	1.32	1.41	1.49	1.58
1.71	0.94	0.97	1.02	1.08	1.15	1.23	1.31	1.39	1.48	1.56
1.72	0.92	0.95	1.00	1.07	1.14	1.21	1.30	1.38	1.46	1.54
1.73	0.90	0.94	0.99	1.05	1.12	1.20	1.28	1.37	1.45	1.53
1.74	0.88	0.92	0.97	1.04	1.11	1.19	1.27	1.35	1.44	1.51
1.75	0.86	0.91	0.96	1.03	1.10	1.18	1.26	1.35	1.42	1.50
1.76	0.85	0.89	0.95	1.02	1.09	1.17	1.26	1.34	1.42	1.49
1.77	0.84	0.88	0.94	1.01	1.09	1.17	1.25	1.33	1.41	1.48
1.78	0.83	0.87	0.94	1.01	1.09	1.17	1.25	1.33	1.40	1.47
1.79	0.82	0.87	0.93	1.00	1.08	1.17	1.25	1.33	1.40	1.47
1.80	0.81	0.86	0.93	1.00	1.08	1.17	1.25	1.33	1.40	1.46
1.81	0.80	0.86	0.93	1.01	1.09	1.17	1.26	1.33	1.40	1.46
1.82	0.80	0.86	0.93	1.01	1.09	1.18	1.26	1.34	1.41	1.46
1.83	0.80	0.86	0.94	1.02	1.10	1.19	1.27	1.35	1.41	1.47
1.84	0.80	0.87	0.94	1.03	1.12	1.20	1.28	1.36	1.42	1.47
1.85	0.81	0.88	0.96	1.04	1.13	1.22	1.30	1.37	1.44	1.48
1.86	0.81	0.89	0.97	1.06	1.15	1.24	1.32	1.39	1.45	1.49
1.87	0.82	0.90	0.99	1.08	1.17	1.26	1.34	1.41	1.47	1.51
1.88	0.83	0.92	1.00	1.10	1.19	1.28	1.36	1.43	1.49	1.52
1.89	0.85	0.93	1.03	1.12	1.22	1.31	1.39	1.46	1.51	1.54
1.90	0.87	0.96	1.05	1.15	1.25	1.34	1.42	1.49	1.54	1.56
1.91	0.89	0.98	1.08	1.19	1.28	1.38	1.46	1.52	1.57	1.59
1.92	0.91	1.01	1.12	1.22	1.32	1.42	1.50	1.56	1.60	1.61
1.93	0.94	1.05	1.15	1.26	1.36	1.46	1.54	1.60	1.64	1.64
1.94	0.98	1.08	1.19	1.31	1.41	1.50	1.58	1.64	1.67	1.68
1.95	1.01	1.12	1.24	1.35	1.46	1.56	1.63	1.69	1.72	1.71

m BMI	37	38	39	Optimal BMI	Minimum Risk
1.55	2.08	2.19	2.30	25.78	1.32
1.56	2.05	2.15	2.26	25.81	1.30
1.57	2.02	2.12	2.23	25.84	1.27
1.58	1.99	2.09	2.19	25.87	1.25
1.59	1.95	2.06	2.16	25.88	1.22
1.60	1.92	2.02	2.12	25.89	1.20
1.61	1.89	1.99	2.09	25.89	1.17
1.62	1.87	1.96	2.05	25.88	1.14
1.63	1.84	1.93	2.02	25.87	1.12
1.64	1.81	1.90	1.99	25.85	1.09
1.65	1.78	1.87	1.95	25.82	1.06
1.66	1.75	1.84	1.92	25.78	1.04
1.67	1.73	1.81	1.89	25.74	1.01
1.68	1.70	1.78	1.86	25.68	0.99
1.69	1.68	1.76	1.83	25.63	0.96
1.70	1.66	1.73	1.80	25.56	0.94
1.71	1.64	1.71	1.77	25.49	0.92
1.72	1.62	1.68	1.74	25.40	0.89
1.73	1.60	1.66	1.72	25.32	0.87
1.74	1.58	1.64	1.69	25.22	0.85
1.75	1.57	1.62	1.66	25.12	0.83
1.76	1.55	1.60	1.64	25.01	0.81
1.77	1.54	1.59	1.62	24.89	0.79
1.78	1.53	1.57	1.60	24.77	0.78
1.79	1.52	1.56	1.58	24.64	0.76
1.80	1.51	1.55	1.56	24.50	0.75
1.81	1.51	1.53	1.54	24.36	0.73
1.82	1.50	1.53	1.53	24.21	0.72
1.83	1.50	1.52	1.51	24.05	0.71
1.84	1.50	1.51	1.50	23.89	0.70
1.85	1.51	1.51	1.49	23.73	0.69
1.86	1.51	1.51	1.48	23.56	0.68
1.87	1.52	1.51	1.47	23.38	0.68
1.88	1.53	1.51	1.46	23.20	0.67
1.89	1.54	1.52	1.46	23.01	0.67
1.90	1.56	1.52	1.45	22.83	0.67
1.91	1.58	1.53	1.45	22.63	0.66
1.92	1.60	1.54	1.45	22.44	0.66
1.93	1.62	1.56	1.45	22.24	0.66
1.94	1.64	1.57	1.45	22.04	0.67
1.95	1.67	1.59	1.46	21.83	0.67

Notes

Chapter 1. The Persistence of Misery in Europe and America before 1900

1. Mitchison 1977; Dublin, Lotka, and Spiegelman 1949; Ashby 1915.

2. Dublin, Lotka, and Spiegelman 1949; United Nations 1953; Stolnitz 1955, 1956; Case et al. 1962.

3. Bernard Harris has pointed out (private communication) that interwar nutrition research, while focusing on diseases linked to specific dietary deficiencies, recognized that inadequate general nutrition led to less than optimum health. For example, John Boyd Orr commented that although poor nutrition might not be marked by starvation or dietary disease, the attendant level of health would be less than the "perfect" health enabled by a "perfectly adequate" diet (Orr 1936, p. 36).

4. Scrimshaw, Taylor, and Gordon 1968. The synergy between nutrition and infection is discussed further in Chapter 3.

5. Flinn 1974; Gille 1949; Bourgeois-Pichat 1965; Henry 1965. Compare Utterström 1965.

6. Toutain 1971; Grantham 1993; Oddy 1990; Shammas 1990; Holderness 1989; Allen 1994; Fogel, Floud, and Harris, n.d.

7. Scrimshaw and Gordon 1968; Fogel 1993.

8. United Nations 1953, 1973.

9. McKeown 1976, 1978; Meeker 1972; Higgs 1973, 1979; Langer 1975; Kunitz 1986; Lee 1980, 1984; Winter 1982; Perrenoud 1984; Fridlizius 1979, 1984; Livi-Bacci 1983, 1991; cf. Razzell 1973. For a balanced assessment of McKeown's contributions from the standpoint of 2002, see Harris 2002.

10. Meuvret 1946, 1965; Goubert 1965; Smith 1977; Flinn 1981; Helleiner 1967; Wrigley 1969; Flinn 1970, 1974; Hoskins 1964, 1968.

11. INED 1977; Wrigley and Schofield 1981; Rebaudo 1979; Dupâquier 1989; Fogel, Floud, and Harris, n.d. I am indebted to Christopher J. Acito for the construction of this figure.

12. United Nations 1973, 1: 142.

13. Lee 1981.

14. United Nations 1973; Lebrun 1971; Flinn 1974, 1981; Blayo 1975b; Wrigley and Schofield 1981; Lee 1981; Weir 1982, 1989; Richards 1984; Galloway 1986; Bengtsson and Ohlsson 1985; cf. Eckstein, Schultz, and Wolpin 1985.

15. Fogel 1997.

16. Fogel, Floud, and Harris, n.d.; cf. Allen 1994.

17. On sleeping vs. nonsleeping BMR, see Bender and Bender 1997; Garrow, James, and Ralph 2000.

18. Bellagio Conference 1983.

19. Quenouille et al. 1951; FAO/WHO/UNU 1985.

20. This table differs somewhat from table 5 in Fogel 1997 because of refinements in the estimates that underlie it.

21. $7,731 \div 17,768 \approx 0.44$.

22. Wrigley 1987.

23. Wrigley 1987; Lindert and Williamson 1982; Fogel, Floud, and Harris, n.d.

24. $105 \div 210 \approx 0.50$.

25. What is involved here is a reduction in leisure-time activities or in domestic activities of individuals not counted in the labor force (e.g., children).

26. Fogel, Floud, and Harris, n.d.

27. Fogel 1986; Costa and Steckel 1997.

28. Fogel 1993 and the sources in Table 1.4.

29. For a further discussion of the disconnect between economic and biomedical measures of the standard of living, see Chapter 2, especially the discussion of the downward adjustments in wage rates needed to correct for economically-induced increases in morbidity and mortality. In this connection, Tanner has pointed out that if children are stunted without having their growth tempo slowed down, it is likely that the stunting is due to insults in fetal life and may be related to the pathology of the placenta. Severe undernutrition or poisoning in early infancy can also lead to permanent stunting (Tanner 1982).

Chapter 2. Why the Twentieth Century Was So Remarkable

1. Part of the wording for this definition was suggested by J. M. Tanner.

2. In this chapter "evolution" is used in two ways. The term "genetic evolution" refers to species change through natural selection among species with different genetic characteristics, some of which are more appropriate to their environment than others. I use the term "technophysio evolution" to refer to changes in human physiology brought about *primarily* by environmental factors. The environmental factors include those influencing physiological and biochemical conditions of the womb in which the embryo and fetus develop. Such environmental factors may be concurrent with the development of the embryo and fetus or they may have occurred prior to the conception of the embryo, either earlier in the life of the mother or higher up in the maternal pedigree. Experimental studies on animal models indicate that environmental insults in the first generation continue to have potency in retarding physiological performance over several generations, despite the absence of subsequent insults, although the potency of the initial insult declines from one generation to another (Chandra 1975, 1992; Meinhold et al. 1993; Fraker et al. 1986). Although final stature is particularly sensitive to insults *in utero* and infancy, insults later in the developmental cycle can also contribute to stunting. It is also worth noting that while only a small proportion of

births in OECD nations today are below 2500 grams, it is likely that 40 to 50 percent of births among workers in England and France in 1800 were below 2500 grams (Fogel 1986).

I italicized primarily to indicate that the potency of particular environmental insults varies from one individual to another in a manner that might reflect complex interactions between environmental and genetic factors. I abstract from the uses of the term "evolution" in embryogenesis and in its use as a bridging function in the principle of recapitulation. On these meanings of the term "evolution" and its general history see Richards 1992 and Mayr 1982.

3. Waaler 1984; Costa and Steckel 1997.

4. Fogel 1993.

5. There are some cancers and other diseases that are positively correlated with height. See Waaler 1984 and Davey Smith et al. 2000.

6. Waaler 1984.

7. See Kim 1996 for the method of estimating Waaler surfaces.

8. Fogel, Floud, and Harris, n.d.

For those interested in the means of calculating these odds, see the Appendix.

This result suggests the importance of cohort factors in the secular decline in mortality. For reviews of the literature on cohort and period effects on the secular decline in mortality rates, see Elo and Preston 1992 and Kuh and Davey Smith 1993.

The decreased importance of changes in human physiology that are correlated with height and weight suggests that other factors, including medical innovations, now matter more. However, this does not mean that height and weight have lost their predictive value. Average heights are still increasing, and inability to maintain adequate BMI is life-threatening for many elderly. Barker (1992, 1998) reports that anthropometric measures at birth predict BMI and hip-to-waist ratios among persons at late middle ages.

9. For a somewhat different view, see Livi-Bacci 1991.

10. Fogel, Costa, and Kim 1993. The curve turns up after 195 cm, suggesting an optimal height.

11. Gould 1869; Centers for Disease Control, unpublished data tables of height in inches and weight in pounds, 1988–94. See Anthropometric

Reference Data, United States, 1988–94, on the Internet at http://www.cdc.gov/nchs/about/major/nhanes/datatblelink.htm.

12. Fogel, Costa, and Kim 1993. In fact, Figure 2.7 underpredicts the improvement in chronic diseases that actually took place. In other words, there were improvements in physiology that are not fully captured by measures of height and weight alone.

13. Cf. Table 4.5. The fact that changes in height and weight predict a decline in chronic conditions does not mean that they caused the decline since these variables may merely be proxies for more fundamental physiological changes that are not directly measured. See Fogel, Floud, and Harris, n.d.

14. Fogel, Costa, and Kim 1993.

15. Fogel, Costa, and Kim 1993.

16. Tanner 1990, 1993.

17. Fogel, Floud, and Harris, n.d.

18. Fogel, Floud, and Harris, n.d.; Fogel 1994.

19. Dasgupta 1993.

20. Computational procedures are sketched in Fogel 1994 and are presented in more detail in Fogel, Floud, and Harris, n.d.

21. Williamson 1976; David and Solar 1977; Gallman and Wallis 1992.

22. Barker 1994, 1998; Costa 1993a, 1993b; Kim 1993.

23. Fogel and Engerman 1971; Gallman 1972; Easterlin 1975; McCutcheon 1992.

24. Boyd 1941; Ackerknecht 1945, [1952] 1965; Smillie 1955.

25. Ackerknecht 1945; Smillie 1955; May 1958; Kunitz 1983; New York State Board of Health 1867.

26. Williamson's application of the bribery principle, using differences in wage rates between regions of high and low mortality to measure the disutility of English industrialization (Williamson 1981a, 1981b, 1982), represents an important advance in the assessment of both the short- and long-run costs and benefits of economic growth during the nineteenth century. The debate set off by his estimates (Pollard 1981; Floud 1984b) involves such issues as whether workers had enough information to properly assess differences in risks, whether the measures of mortality used by Williamson were precise enough to gauge

the differential risks that workers actually suffered in particular occupations and localities, and whether the various labor markets were
all in equilibrium (or all out of equilibrium by the same degree). The
resolution of these issues will no doubt add greatly to our knowledge
about the costs and benefits of industrialization to the workers who
experienced it.

Alternative approaches to the computation of the mortality correction have been proposed (Usher 1973, 1980; Williamson 1984;
Lindert 1986). Still another approach is suggested by equation (1),
which is derived from the theory of human capital:

$$w_n = (i + \delta_n)V_n \tag{1}$$

where

$w_n =$ the wage rate at age n of a worker

$i \;\;=$ the market rate of return on capital

$\delta_n =$ the annual rate of depreciation in the stock of human capital
at age n (the probability of dying between age n and $n + 1$)

$V_n =$ the cost of producing a new worker aged n (the long-run
equilibrium price of such a worker if he could be sold as a
slave)

Differentiating equation (1) totally yields

$$\overset{*}{w_n} = \phi \overset{*}{i} + (1 - \phi)\overset{*}{\delta_n} + \overset{*}{V_n} \tag{2}$$

where

$\phi = [i/(i + \delta_n)]$

$* =$ an asterisk over a variable indicates the rate of change in that
variable

Equations (1) and (2) indicate that increases in mortality rates will
lead to spurious increases both in "real" wages (wages adjusted only
for the price level) and in "real" per capita income. That is because
conventional measures of real wages and per capita income fail to
distinguish between rises in wages that are due to, say, technological
change and those that are due to a more rapid consumption of human
capital, treating both as if they represented net additions to human
welfare. Equations (1) and (2) indicate that increased mortality rates

raise wages not only because they increase δ (the probability that someone in the labor force will die), but also because they increase V (the cost of producing a new entrant into the labor force). The higher the mortality rate, the greater the number of live births (and associated costs) needed to produce a new entrant into the labor force. There is, of course, a corresponding increase in cost due to extra expenditures on nonsurvivors at all the other ages between birth and entry into the labor force.

The estimates of $\overset{*}{\delta}$ and $\overset{*}{V}$, which can be derived from the decline in life expectancy shown in Figure 1.2 (cf. Fogel 1986), indicate that rising mortality may have accounted for about two-fifths of the average annual increase in the conventional measure of real per capita income over the 70 years between 1790 and 1860. In principle, this correction is a lower bound on the correction that one would obtain from the proper implementation of the bribery principle, since no account was taken of the psychic cost involved in the loss of loved ones, since increases in morbidity and other deterioration in the quality of life and capacity to work are not measured, and since it was implicitly assumed that workers were risk neutral with respect to their own fate.

The preceding estimate is merely meant to illustrate the improvements in measured income made possible by the fuller incorporation of biomedical variables into economic analysis. Work now underway with stature and BMI is providing additional information, beyond that conveyed by the mortality series, because these variables pertain to the quality of life of individuals who lived under changing mortality regimens. Although the calculation based on equation (1) suggested the magnitude of the correction needed to net out the effect of rises in mortality rates on conventional measures of per capita income, it did not provide adjustments for the consequences of increased morbidity rates experienced by those who survived exposure to virulent diseases. Such corrections are needed to take account of medical expenditures and a variety of investments that merely offset the deterioration in the environment, and of diseases that degraded the quality of life and reduced the productivity of the labor of survivors. The data on stature and BMI promise to provide such adjustments (Floud 1984a; Costa 1998, 1993a, 1993b; Kim 1993; Steckel 1995).

27. Kuznets 1952.

28. Floud, Wachter, and Gregory 1990.

29. Consider, for example, the food that gave the upper classes their superior diet and the housing that reduced their exposure to disease.
If the nutrients were sold to them by a perfectly discriminating mo-
nopolist, the benefits they derived in improved health would have
been incorporated in the price of the nutrients. However, food was
sold in a competitive market. Similarly, the value of the extra health
benefits that accrued to the rich because of the nature of their housing could not be captured by the laborers who built the houses or
by the brickmakers who sold their wares competitively, nor could it
be fully captured by the landowners. Since there was an excess supply of land with the quality called "separated from reservoirs of disease," landowners could usually only capture conventional benefits of
proximity.

30. Case et al. 1962; Haines 1979; U.S. Public Health Service 1963.

31. Williamson and Lindert 1980; Phelps Brown 1988; Perkin 1990.

32. U.S. Bureau of the Census 1975; Karpinos 1958. For somewhat different views on these issues, see Preston 1975, Preston and van de
Walle 1978, and McKeown 1976 and 1979.

33. Contemporary commentators often deal with differentials by social
class as though they are greater today than they have ever been. This
is merely an expression of their unfamiliarity with the work of historical epidemiologists and demographers. For further details, see Fogel
2000.

34. In this calculation and in the one that follows, I have ignored possible
changes in average commuting times since it is difficult to estimate
whether the average time needed to get to and from work has increased or decreased since 1860. Although the average distance has
probably increased, the speed of transportation has also increased.

35. Fogel 2000. It must be noted that not all extra leisure has been con-
structively employed. The twentieth century, particularly the last few
decades, experienced sharp increases in such unmeasured costs as
crime, drug use, and threats to safety that significantly offset unmeasured benefits.

    Another implication of this line of argument is that the inequality
of the international distribution of income is greater than is indicated
by current conventions for comparing the income of nations. The

human development index (United Nations 1990) may overcome some of these deficiencies by giving explicit recognition to life expectancy (but not to the level of morbidity) and by including a measure of education. However, there is reason to doubt whether schooling by itself adequately captures the wide disparities in both the quantity and quality of leisure.

36. Stature and Gini ratios are significantly correlated, but as the following discussion of height and BMI indicates, the anthropometric measures reveal important aspects of welfare that are not as apparent in the movement of Gini ratios.

37. There has been a rise in the Gini ratio since 1973 in virtually all the rich nations for which such information is available. Cf. Fogel 2000.

38. On trends in the Gini ratio between c. 1690 and 1973 and the debate over this trend, see Soltow 1968; Feinstein 1988; Williamson 1981a, 1985; Lindert and Williamson 1982, 1983; Floud, Wachter, and Gregory 1990. Cf. Fogel 2000.

39. Data for males are presented in Case et al. 1962; Hollingsworth 1977; Hattersley 1999.

40. Steckel 1995; Rona, Swan, and Altman 1978.

41. Fogel 1992; cf. van Wieringen 1986; Drukker 1994; Drukker and Tassenaar 1997; Schmidt, Jorgenson, and Michaelsen 1995.

42. Cipolla 1980; Laslett [1965] 1984; Himmelfarb 1983; Soltow 1968; Lindert and Williamson 1982; Fogel 1987, 1989, 1993; Colquhoun 1814; Hannon 1984a, 1984b, 1985; Jencks 1994.

43. Fogel 1997; Fogel, Floud, and Harris, n.d.

Chapter 3. Tragedies and Miracles in the Third World

1. Kiple 1993.

2. The doubly labeled water method, which provides a metabolic measure of energy expenditure, has shown that food diaries systematically underestimate average food consumption. Results from national food balance sheets are close to those obtained from using the doubly labeled water method. See Schoeller 1990; Black et al. 1996; Black and Cole 2000.

3. Equations were worked out relating the energy requirement for basal metabolism to specific climatic conditions and to the height, weight,

and surface areas of individuals. See, for example, Quenouille et al. 1951.

4. United Nations 1953, 1973; FAO/WHO/UNU 1985.

5. The extreme manifestations of PEM are called "kwashiorkor" and "marasmus." Both diseases involve severe wasting of body tissue; kwashiorkor is also characterized by edema (Waterlow, Tomkins, and Grantham-McGregor 1992).

6. Sommer and Lowenstein 1975; Chen, Chowdhury, and Huffman 1980; Billewicz and MacGregor 1982; Kielmann et al. 1983; Martorell 1985.

7. A number of statistical criticisms were also raised with respect to methods used to establish the caloric threshold of malnutrition, as well as to the use of household diaries to relate the prevalence of malnutrition to income levels. See Osmani 1992a; Srinivasan 1992; Dasgupta 1993.

8. See Gopalan, Payne, Osmani, and Srinivasan, among others, in Osmani 1992b; see also Sukhatme 1982. It was argued that even if Western standards did not exaggerate the extent of stunting and wasting in Asia, the FAWOB analysis did not address the costs of being small. The evidence showing that small individuals were more likely to suffer illness was challenged, as was the evidence on the nexus to severity of illness. The claim that large people were more productive than small ones was also contested.

9. Agarwal et al. 1991.

10. The Dutch growth centiles are computed from 1985 data analyzed by Roede and van Wieringen 1985 and also reported in Eveleth and Tanner 1990. The observations of adolescent English boys are collected from a variety of sources identified in Fogel, Floud, and Harris, n.d. I am indebted to Professor Floud, who assembled these observations.

11. The shortfall is about half a standard deviation.

12. On the British see Floud, Wachter, and Gregory 1990; on the Americans see Costa and Steckel 1997; on the Dutch see van Wieringen 1986.

13. Maddison 1995.

14. Landes 1969, 1998.

15. New York City Department of Health 1871, pp. 315–16.

16. Warren 2000; Aggett and Comerford 1995.

17. Goubert 1984.

18. U.S. Bureau of the Census 1975; Raper, Zizza, and Rourke 1992.

19. As a result, life expectancy at birth increased far more rapidly in Third World countries than in the industrialized countries of Europe. In India, for example, life expectancy at birth increased from 29 years in 1930 to 60 years in 1990. An increase of that magnitude required two and a half centuries in England and France. The sharp drop in the death rates of developing nations led to an enormous surge in the growth of population, which in turn led to widespread fears that the food supply could not keep up with population growth and that industrialization would be thwarted. However, none of these forecasts turned out to be true (Carr-Saunders 1964; World Bank 1992, 1993; Wrigley and Schofield 1981; Keyfitz and Flieger 1968, 1990; Weir 1989; Dublin and Lotka 1936; Kuznets 1971. See also Kelley and Williamson 1983).

20. Sen 1981.

21. World Bank 1992, Table 28.

  I am indebted to Jesse Ausubel of the Rockefeller University for the following data computed from FAOSTAT <http://apps.fao.org/>:

Percent Change per Year in the Food Supply,
1961–2000

	Calories per Day per Capita	Protein (Grams) per Day per Capita
Crop	0.56	0.50
Animal	0.78	0.92
Total	0.59	0.61

Furthermore, while the weight of cereals per capita has increased by 0.46 percent per year during the same time period, the quality weighted production index number has risen by 0.66 percent per year, indicating that the consumption of hiqh-quality protein, such as that from meat, eggs, and dairy products, has outpaced the consumption of lower-quality protein from crops (e.g., wheat and rye). These increases have occurred despite a concurrent 1.46 percent per year decrease in the hectares of arable and permanent crops per capita. As Ausubel has also noted, this improvement in the food supply manifests a higher income elasticity of demand for animal protein than for calories (private communication, 30 Nov. 2002).

22. FAO 1996.

23. Sukhatme 1982; cf. Black and Cole 2000; Black et al. 1996.

24. This finding, incidentally, contradicts the contention that the left-hand part of the Waaler curves in BMIs is attributable primarily to smoking, since smoking was much less common in the 1890s than it is today.

   Kim examined a succession of NHIS surveys between 1982 and 1992. Although the results are sensitive to the method of curve fitting, he concluded that the curve of optimal weight, for given heights, appears to have been stable over these years (Kim 1995).

25. As successive generations increase in height, their location on the line of optimal height on Figure 2.4 will move toward increasingly lower risk levels.

26. The slowdown in the increase in height in the Netherlands, the United States, and some other countries does not necessarily mean that the secular increase has come to an end, since, as Figure 1.2 illustrates, such slowdowns, or even reversals, occurred in the past without marking the end of the secular increase.

27. There is no compelling evidence to contradict the assumption that the difference between current Dutch and U.S. stature is due primarily to technophysio evolution rather than to genetic factors. In the 1860s the average height of Dutch males at maturity was 8 cm less than that of U.S. males, and the Dutch did not exceed average U.S. heights until after World War II (van Wieringen 1986).

28. Cf. Dasgupta 1993.

29. See Costa 1996; Lee 1995.

30. See Fogel, Floud, and Harris, n.d.

31. Computed for a male between ages 30 and 60, with an original BMI of 19 and a stature of 164 cm, on the assumption that the reduction in caloric intake was entirely in the basal metabolic rate (i.e., that the energy devoted to work was undiminished) and that BMR was

originally 60 percent of total energy requirements. The equation used to calculate the reduction in BMR is that reported in FAO/WHO/UNU 1985, Table 5. An alternative and more precise equation is given in Quenouille et al. 1951. The change in risk is computed from Fogel 1993, Table A2. It should be noted that a 5 percent reduction in height and BMI implies a 14 percent reduction in weight. In this case, the indicated adjustments in height and BMI were the equilibrating response to a 4 percent reduction in the food supply. However, if the energy devoted to work is undiminished, a 7 percent reduction in BMR is required.

Chapter 4. Prospects for the Twenty-First Century

1. On anxiety about declining hours of work in the late twentieth century, see, e.g., Rifkin 1995 and Aronowitz and DiFazio 1994. They, along with numerous writers in the popular press, attribute reduced work hours to the malfunctioning of technology. Workers are being displaced by machines. The anxiety is fed by politicians and commentators who looked to the revenue from increased employment as a solution to pension and health care problems.

2. Fogel 2000.

3. Rifkin 1995; Aronowitz and DiFazio 1994.

4. Fogel 2000.

5. Davidson 1982, chap. 9.

6. Robinson 1988; Moffit 1968–92.

7. Veblen [1899] 1934.

8. Shaw [1928] 1931, p. 91.

9. Lee 1996.

10. U.S. Department of Labor, Bureau of Labor Statistics 1994; U.S. Bureau of the Census 1996, pp. 623, 723.

11. U.S. Department of Labor, Bureau of Labor Statistics 1994; U.S. Bureau of the Census 1994; Edmondson 1996; U.S Bureau of the Census 1996, p. 623.

12. U.S. Department of Labor Statistics 1959; U.S. Department of Labor, Bureau of Labor Statistics 1994; Cox and Alm 1998.

13. Goldin 1990.

14. Marks 1995.

15. Shellenbarger 1997; Graham and Crossen 1996.

16. Bohl 1996; Capowski 1996; Peak 1996; Scott 1996.

17. Moffit 1968–92; U.S. Bureau of the Census 1994; Robinson and Godbey 1997; cf. Schor 1991; Hochschild 1997; Lee 2000.

18. Manton 1993; Manton, Corder, and Stallard 1997.

19. Even among households in which both the husband and wife are in the labor force, total hours of work (in the market and as chores at home) are substantially less than they were a century ago. Moreover, families with the highest number of hours (usually between ages 50 and 54) are often trading current leisure for early retirement. See Fogel 2000.

20. Maddison 1991, 1995, 2001.

21. Fogel 2000, chap. 5.

22. See Fogel 2000, Appendix 5D, for the calculations on which this example is based.

23. Iyer 1993; Poortvliet and Laine 1995.

24. Fogel 2000, Appendix 5D.

25. U.S. Social Security Administration 1997.

26. Birch 1974.

27. Cf. *Economic report of the President* 2002.

28. Fogel 2000; cf. Kotlikoff 1996.

29. Laslett 1991; Lenk 1994.

30. Improvements in the efficiency of delivering health services as well as improvements in the quality of health care have actually reduced the price of health care services once account is taken of quality. Similarly, the Internet has reduced the cost of acquiring information.

31. Computed from unpublished data in the Union Army and Health and Retirement Study samples; see also Bell, Wade, and Goss 1992.

32. Barker 1998.

33. Law and Shiell 1996; Frankel et al. 1996; Scrimshaw 1997; Leon et al. 1998. For more detail, see Chapter 5.

34. Manton and Gu 2001.

35. Murray and Lopez 1996.

36. Work on the National Long-Term Care Survey has revealed an accelerating decline in disability rates since the early 1980s. See Manton, Corder, and Stallard 1997; Singer and Manton 1998; Manton and Gu 2001; Jacobzone 2002.
37. Cutler and Meara 1998.
38. Newhouse 2001; Duggan 2000; Chernichovsky 2000.
39. Keyfitz and Flieger 1990.
40. Fogel 2000 and 2003.
41. *Statistical yearbook of China* 2001; World Bank 2001.
42. Keyfitz and Flieger 1990.

Chapter 5. Problems of Equity in Health Care

1. See, for example, Pappas et al. 1993; Ecob and Davey Smith 1999; Boorah 1999; Tüchsen and Endahl 1999; Michelozzi et al. 1999; Schuller 1999; Liu, Hsiao, and Eggleston 1999.
2. WHO 2000, p. xiii.
3. WHO 2000, p. xviii.
4. WHO 2000; Hurst 2000.
5. Manton, Stallard, and Corder 1997; van Poppel and van der Heijden 1997; Barker 1998; Fogel 2000.
6. Cresswell et al. 1997; Barker 1997; Henry et al. 1997; Ravelli et al. 1998; Scrimshaw 1997; Barker and Martyn 1997; Andersson et al. 1997.
7. Law and Shiell 1996.
8. Law and Shiell 1996; Frankel et al. 1996; Koupilová, Leon, and Vågerö 1997; Leon et al. 1998; Forsén et al. 1997; Stein et al. 1996, 1997.
9. Paneth and Susser 1995; Perry et al. 1995; Scrimshaw 1997.
   This evidence strongly suggests that environmental influences continue to dominate the pattern of improvement in chronic conditions at later ages. However, the evidence needed to document the proposition is not yet in hand. The Center for Population Economics at the University of Chicago has recently begun collecting data needed to measure the impact of improvements to the environment on the decline in disabilities during the twentieth century (the EXDID Project).

10. Doblhammer and Vaupel 2001.

11. Kanjanapipatkul 2001.

12. World Health Organization, Commission on Macroeconomics and Health (WHO/CMH) 2001, p. 42.

13. WHO/CMH 2001, p. 42.

14. WHO/CMH 2001, p. 18; World Bank 2001, Table 1.

15. The Blair administration has made the reduction in waiting times for the treatment of nonemergency conditions a priority. Lyall 1999.

16. Hurst 2000; Sekhri 2000.

17. U.S. Census Bureau 2000a, Table 194; World Health Organization, Regional Office for Europe 1997, p. 35; Organization for Economic Co-operation and Development 2001.

18. Sekhri 2000.

19. Fogel 2000. The income elasticity of the demand for cars in the U.S. between 1910 and 1970 was 2.6 (Fogel 1999).

20. Berk and Schur 1998; Freeman et al. 1990; Perry and Rosen 2001.

21. Beale 2001; Malmström, Sundquist, and Johansson 1999.

22. Shah-Canning, Alpert, and Bauchner 1996; Fronstin 2000; Douglass and Torres 1994; Wallihan, Stump, and Callahan 1999; Freeman and Corey 1993.

23. Keyfitz and Flieger 1990; World Bank 1997.

24. WHO/CMH 2001.

Postscript: How Long Can We Live?

1. U.S. Census Bureau 2000b.

2. Change in the age structure accounts for some of the change in the distribution of deaths. According to this proposition, countries in which this decline has already occurred are unlikely to be able to produce another such reduction in mortality rates. U.S. National Center for Health Statistics 1997; Preston, Keyfitz, and Schoen 1972; Preston 1985; Linder and Grove 1947.

3. Oeppen and Vaupel 2002.

4. Dublin 1928; Dublin and Lotka 1936.

5. Fries 1980, 1990.

6. See Oeppen and Vaupel 2002 suppl.

7. Helmchen 2003; Charlson et al. 1994; Stuck et al. 1999; Manton and Gu 2001.

8. Costa, forthcoming.

9. Helmchen 2003.

10. Arnst 2003.

11. *Economist* 2003.

Appendix

1. Kim subsequently obtained the Norwegian data set of approximately 1.8 million observations. The plots of Waaler surfaces obtained from the disaggregated data were virtually the same as those shown in this book. However, with the full set of observations, many additional issues could be addressed. See Kim 1996.

Glossary of Technical Terms

anthropometric data: physical measurements of the human body, such as standing height, sitting height, weight, and skinfold thickness.

autoimmune thyroiditis: an inflammation of the thyroid gland commonly caused by an abnormal immune response in which lymphocytes (white blood cells that generally fight infection and disease) invade the tissues of the gland.

basal metabolism: the minimum amount of energy expended by the body to maintain vital processes, such as respiration, circulation, digestion, and body temperature.

beriberi: a nutritional disorder due to deficiency of vitamin B_1. It is widespread in rice-eating communities in which the diet is based on polished rice from which the seed coat has been removed.

biodemography: the statistical study of human populations, especially with reference to size and density, distribution, vital statistics, health, and life processes.

biomedical data: includes anthropometric data as well as vital rates and physiological characteristics.

body build: synonym for the shape of the body, referring to such descriptors as height, weight, muscle development, percentage of weight due to lean body mass, and so on.

body mass: synonym for BMI.

body mass index (BMI): a measure of body fat determined by weight in kilograms divided by height in meters squared and generally adjusted for gender and age. For most adults, it is a good indicator of underweight or obesity, but it may not be accurate for highly athletic persons with large amounts of lean muscle mass.

cholera: an acute infection of the small intestine by the bacterium *Vibrio cholerae*, which causes severe vomiting and diarrhea leading to dehydration. If the dehydration is not reversed, the disease can lead to death in a short time. The disease is contracted from food or drinking water contaminated by feces.

concentration ratio: a synonym for the Gini ratio.

consumer durables: goods that are relatively expensive, such as automobiles, TV sets, and washing machines, which yield services or utility over time rather than being completely used up at the moment of consumption.

consuming unit: the number of calories consumed on average by a male aged 20–39. Used to standardize caloric consumption across the age and sex distributions of a population.

coronary heart disease: narrowing of the blood vessels of the heart, usually due to fat or cholesterol deposits in the arteries.

demography: the branch of the social sciences concerned with vital rates such as death rates, birth rates, and morbidity rates.

GDP: gross domestic product. GDP is a monetary value of all the goods and services produced by an economy over a specified period. It is measured in three ways: (1) on the basis of expenditure, (2) on the basis of income, (3) on the basis of the value added by each industry. It is currently the most common measure of the material income of a country.

Gini ratio: a coefficient based on the Lorenz curve. The Lorenz curve, in general, is a diagram illustrating the degree of inequality and concentration of income for a group, created by plotting the cumulative percentage of a total income obtained by the cumulative percentages of the group. The Gini ratio represents the degree of inequality in a frequency distribution, such as personal incomes. It varies between 0 (perfect equality) and 1 (perfect inequality).

hernia: the protrusion of an organ or tissue through the wall of the body cavity in which it normally lies.

heterosis: the marked vigor or capacity for growth often exhibited by crossbred animals or plants; also called *hybrid vigor*.

humoral antibodies: antibodies (white blood cells that target and fight infections) that circulate in the blood.

hypertension: high blood pressure.

in utero: in the womb.

income elasticity: the proportionate change in the quantity of a commodity demanded after a unit proportionate change in the income of consumers, with prices held constant.

leisure class: a term used by Thorstein Veblen (1857–1929) in his book *The Theory of the Leisure Class* (1899) to identify a group of consumers with ostentatious personal spending that satisfies no physical need but rather a psychological need for the esteem of others. Goods may be purchased not for their practical use but as "status symbols" and to "keep up with the Joneses."

Malthus, Malthusian-type famines: Thomas Robert Malthus (1766–1834) is generally remembered for his essays on population. Malthus argued that population has a natural growth rate described by a geometric progression and that natural resources necessary to support the population grew at a rate similar to an arithmetic progression. He thought that without restraints on fertility there would be continued pressure on living standards and eventual overpopulation leading to famine.

metabolism: the sum of all the chemical and physical changes that take place within the body and enable its continued growth and functioning.

morbidity: the state of being diseased.

mortality: the incidence of death in a population during a given period.

national income: the total incomes of residents of an economy in a given period after providing for capital consumption (the replacement value of capital used up in the process of production). National income is regarded as an indicator of national welfare in the market economy. See also **GDP.**

NIPA (national income and product accounts): the official government system, maintained by the Bureau of Economic Analysis in the Department of Commerce, for collecting, processing, and reporting assorted production and income measures used to track aggregate activity in the macroeconomy. The NIPA is the source of official estimates of gross domestic product, net domestic product, national income, personal income, disposable income, gross national product, and related measures.

OECD nations: nations belonging to the Organization for Economic Cooperation and Development. The OECD came into being in 1961. Its aims are (1) to encourage economic growth and high employment with financial stability among member countries and (2) to contribute to the economic development of the less advanced member and non-member countries and the expansion of world multilateral trade. The OECD has become particularly important as a forum for the industrialized countries to discuss international monetary problems and to promote aid and technical assistance for developing countries.

pathogen: a microorganism, such as a bacterium, that invades an animal (or plant) or human and produces disease.

pellagra: a nutritional disease due to a deficiency of nicotinic acid (a B vitamin) that results from the consumption of a diet that is poor in either nicotinic acid or tryptophan.

phagocytosis: the engulfment and digestion of bacteria and other foreign particles by a cell.

present value: the current net value of an investment project; used to compare the net benefits and costs of investment projects, taking into account the rate of interest.

real terms: a money value adjusted for changes in the price level. To convert money values to constant prices or real terms, it is necessary to deflate data at current prices by an appropriate index number.

real wages: see **real terms.**

rickets: a disease of childhood in which the bones do not harden due to a deficiency of vitamin D.

scurvy: a disease caused by a deficiency of vitamin C.

stroke: a sudden attack of weakness affecting one side of the body as a consequence of an interruption to the flow of blood to the brain.

type II diabetes: also known as "non-insulin-dependent diabetes" or "adult-onset diabetes." Diabetes is a disorder of carbohydrate metabolism in which sugars in the body are not oxidized to produce energy due to lack of the pancreatic hormone insulin. Type II diabetes is the most common form of diabetes and accounts for approximately 90–95 percent of all cases of the disease.

Biographical Notes

WILBUR O. ATWATER (1844–1907) received his Ph.D. from Yale in 1869 for studies on the chemical composition of corn. Studying in Berlin and Leipzig, he became familiar with German techniques for measuring respiration and metabolism, and used these techniques to conduct studies on food analysis, dietary evaluations, energy requirements for work, digestibility of foods, and the economics of food production. He recommended controlled dietary studies to determine how nutrient intake affected metabolism and muscular effort. Most diet analysis programs currently incorporate Atwater's databases of food composition values.

RODERICK FLOUD (1942–) received his Ph.D. from Oxford in 1970 and was Professor of Modern History at Birkbeck College in London from 1975 to 1988. He is presently Vice-Chancellor of London Metropolitan University. He has authored and edited many books on history and economics, including *The Economic History of Britain since 1700* and *Health and Welfare during Industrialisation* (1997).

SIMON KUZNETS (1901–85) received his Ph.D. from Columbia University in 1926. Kuznets taught at the University of Pennsylvania from 1930 to 1954, at Johns Hopkins University from 1954 until 1960, and at Harvard University from 1960 until his retirement in 1971. He was awarded the Nobel Prize in Economics in 1971 for his contribution to the measurement and analysis of economic growth. He was on staff at the National Bureau of Economic Research from 1927 to 1961, where he pioneered in the development of national income accounts. His publications include *Secular Movements in Production and Prices* (1930), *National Income and Its Composition, 1919–1938* (1941), *Economic Growth and Structure* (1965), and *Population, Capital, and Growth* (1979).

RONALD LEE (1941–) received his M.A. in Demography from the University of California at Berkeley and his Ph.D. in Economics from Harvard in 1971, and then spent a postdoctoral year at INED, the French National Demographic Institute. He taught in the Economics Department at the University of Michigan for 8 years, and then went to UC Berkeley, where he is presently Professor of Demography and Economics and Director of the Center on the Economics and Demography of Aging. He has authored and edited numerous books and articles on demography and aging. He is a past president of the Population Association of America and received the Mindel Shepps Award for outstanding research in mathematical demography and demographic methods. He is a member of the National Academy of Sciences and a Corresponding Member of the British Academy.

THOMAS MCKEOWN (1911–1988) received his Ph.D. from Cambridge University and from 1950 to 1978 was Professor of Social Medicine at the University of Birmingham Medical School. He was a major historian of medicine and put forth the influential and controversial McKeown Thesis, which argued that the growth in world population after 1700 was not due primarily to the increase in lifesaving medicine or public health policies, but rather to improvements in overall standards of living resulting from better economic conditions, especially nutrition.

JEAN MEUVRET (1901–1971) was a historian of early modern France. He was a tutor at the Ecole Normale Supérieure and was known in Europe and America for his pioneering studies of the French economy in the seventeenth century. His most important work, *Le problème des subsistances à l'époque de Louis XIV* (3 vols., 1977–88), examines the corn economy of France during the Old Regime. Meuvret was interested in showing how historical conditions affected different networks or circuits of exchange in an early monetary economy.

ROGER SNOWDEN SCHOFIELD (1937–) received his Ph.D. from Cambridge University in 1963. He is a Fellow of Clare College, Cambridge, and was Honorary Reader in Historical Demography at Cambridge from 1991 to 1998. His books include *The Population History of England, 1541–1871: A Reconstruction* (with E. A. Wrigley, 1981), *Famine, Disease and the Social Order in Early Modern Society* (1989), and *English Population History from Family Reconstitutions 1580–1837* (with others, 1997).

THEODORE SCHULTZ (1902–1998) received his Ph.D. from the University of Wisconsin in Economics and in 1943 accepted a chair in Economics at the University of Chicago, where he remained until his retirement in 1974. He was awarded the Nobel Prize in Economics in 1979 (jointly with Sir William Arthur Lewis). His major publications include *Agriculture in an Unstable Economy* (1953), *The Economic Organization of Agriculture* (1953), *Transforming Traditional Agriculture* (1964), and *Investment in Human Capital: The Role of Education and Research* (1971). Schultz developed the ideas of human-capital theory in his work on the economics of education and made major contributions to the analysis of agriculture in developing countries. He highlighted the distortion of policy in taxation and trade that biases development against agriculture, condemning the sector to subsistence farming.

P. V. SUKHATME (1911–1997) received his Ph.D. in 1939 from the University of London, specializing in food and nutrition. He was a Fellow of the American Statistical Association and the National Academy of Sciences of India. He was influential in the field of statistics and statistical methods for agriculture and food production in India and Southeast Asia. His works include *Statistical Methods for Agricultural Workers* (1954), *Feeding India's Growing Millions* (1965), and *The World's Hunger* (1961). During the 1970s and 1980s he also worked with WHO on topics such as agricultural productivity and the use and safety of irradiated foods.

HANS TH. WAALER although originally trained as an economist, spent his career as an epidemiologist. Perhaps the best known of his many papers is a monograph entitled "Height, Weight and Mortality: The Norwegian Experience." At the time of its publication, this pathbreaking study of 1.8 million persons included the largest dataset ever used to evaluate mortality as a function of body build. Waaler also called to public attention the U-shaped pattern of mortality with respect to BMI and the reverse J-shaped pattern of the relationship between mortality and height. He was the first to draw iso-risk curves relating both body height and body weight to the odds of dying. Until his retirement, Waaler was an investigator at the National Institute of Public Health in Oslo.

SIR EDWARD ANTHONY WRIGLEY (1931–) received his Ph.D. in Geography from Cambridge University in 1957 and was Master of Corpus Christi College. He is the cofounder of the Cambridge Group for the History of Population and Social Structure and from 1997 to 2001 was President of the British Academy. Wrigley has written extensively on the population history of England between the mid-sixteenth and mid-nineteenth centuries and on the relationship between short-term and secular changes in major economic and demographic variables during this period. His works and edited volumes include *Industrial Growth and Population Change* (1961), *Population and History* (1969), *The Population History of England, 1541–1871: A Reconstruction* (with Roger Schofield, 1981), *The Works of Thomas Malthus* (1986), and *English Population History from Family Reconstitution, 1580–1837* (with others, 1997).

References

Ackernecht, E. H. 1945, *Malaria in the upper Mississippi Valley, 1760–1900*, Baltimore: Johns Hopkins University Press.

Ackernecht, E. H. [1952] 1965, Diseases in the Middle West, in *Essays in the history of medicine in honor of David J. Davis, M.D., Ph.D. The first ten lectures of the Davis Memorial Lecture Series, University of Illinois College of Medicine*, pp. 168–81, Chicago: University of Illinois Press for the Davis Lecture Committee.

Agarwal, K. N., Agarwal, D. K., Benakappa, D. G., Gupta, S. M., Khanduja, P. C., Khatua, S. P., Ramachandran, K., Udani, P. M., and Gopalan, C. 1991, *Growth performance of affluent Indian children (under-fives)*, New Delhi: Nutrition Foundation of India.

Aggett, P. J. and Comerford, J. G. 1995, Zinc and human health, *Nutrition Reviews* 9: S16–S22.

Allen, R. C. 1992, *Enclosure and the yeoman: The agricultural development of the South Midlands 1450–1850*, Oxford: Oxford University Press.

Allen, R. C. 1994, Agriculture during the industrial revolution, in *The economic history of Britain since 1700*, vol. 1, *1700–1860*, Floud, R.

and McCloskey, D. (eds.), 2d ed., pp. 96–122, Cambridge: Cambridge University Press.

Andersson, S.-O., Wolk, A., Bergström, R., Adami, H.-O., Engholm, G., Englund, A., and Nyrén, O. 1997, Body size and prostate cancer: A 20-year follow-up study among 135,006 Swedish construction workers, *Journal of the National Cancer Institute* 89: 385–89.

Arnst, C. 2003, Off-the-shelf body parts, *Business Week* (18–25 Aug.): 106–7.

Aronowitz, S. and DiFazio, W. 1994, *The jobless future: Sci-tech and the dogma of work*, Minneapolis: University of Minnesota Press.

Ashby, H. T. 1915, *Infant mortality*, Cambridge: Cambridge University Press.

Barker, D. J. P. (ed.) 1992, *Fetal and infant origins of adult disease*, London: *British Medical Journal*.

Barker, D. J. P. (ed.) 1994, *Mothers, babies, and disease in later life*, London: BMJ Publishing Group.

Barker, D. J. P. 1997, Fetal nutrition and cardiovascular disease in later life, *British Medical Bulletin* 53: 96–108.

Barker, D. J. P. 1998, *Mothers, babies, and health in later life*, 2d ed., Edinburgh: Churchill Livingstone.

Barker, D. J. P. and Martyn, C. 1997, The fetal origins of hypertension, *Advances in Nephrology from the Necker Hospital* 26: 65–72.

Baxter, J. H. 1875, *Statistics, medical and anthropological, of the Provost-Marshal-General's Bureau, derived from records of the examination for military service in the armies of the United States during the late War of the Rebellion, of over a million recruits, drafted men, substitutes, and enrolled men*, Washington, D.C.: U.S. Government Printing Office.

Beale, N. 2001, Unequal to the task: Deprivation, health and UK general practice at the millennium, *British Journal of General Practice* 51: 478–85.

Bell, A., Wade, H., and Goss, C. 1992, *Life tables for the United States Social Security area: 1900–2080*, Actuarial Study No. 107, Baltimore: U.S. Department of Health and Human Services, Social Security Administration, Office of the Actuary.

Bellagio Conference 1983, The relationship of nutrition, disease, and social conditions: A graphical presentation, in *Hunger and history* [= *Journal of Interdisciplinary History* 14, no. 2]: 503–6.

Bender, D. A. and Bender, A. E. 1997, *Nutrition: A reference handbook*, Oxford: Oxford University Press.

Bengtsson, T. and Ohlsson, R. 1985, Age-specific mortality and short-term changes in the standard of living: Sweden, 1751–1859, *European Journal of Population* 1: 309–26.

Berk, M. L. and Schur, C. L. 1998, Access to care: How much difference does Medicare make? *Health Affairs* 17: 169–80.

Billewicz, W. A. and MacGregor, I. A. 1982, A birth to maturity longitudinal study of heights and weights in two West African (Gambian) villages, *Annals of Human Biology* 9: 309–20.

Birch, R. C. 1974, *The shaping of the welfare state*, Seminar Studies in History, London: Longman.

Black, A. E. and Cole, T. J. 2000, Within- and between-subject variation in energy expenditure measured by the doubly-labelled water technique: Implications for validating reported dietary energy intake, *European Journal of Clinical Nutrition* 54: 386–94.

Black, A. E., Coward, W. A., Cole, T. J., and Prentice, A. M. 1996, Human energy expenditure in affluent societies: An analysis of 574 doubly-labelled water measurements, *European Journal of Clinical Nutrition* 50: 72–92.

Blayo, Y. 1975a, La mortalité en France, *Population* 30 (Numéro Spécial): 123–42.

Blayo, Y. 1975b, Mouvement naturel de la population française de 1740 à 1829, *Population* 30 (Numéro Spécial): 15–64.

Bohl, D. 1996, Mini survey: Companies attempt to create the 'convenient workplace', *Compensation and Benefits Review* 28: 23–26.

Boorah, V. K. 1999, Occupational class and the probability of long-term limiting illness, *Social Science and Medicine* 49: 253–66.

Bourgeois-Pichat, J. 1965, The general development of the population of France since the eighteenth century, in *Population in history: Essays in historical demography*, Glass, D. V. and Eversley, D. E. C. (eds.), pp. 474–506, Chicago: Aldine.

Boyd, M. F. 1941, An historical sketch of the prevalence of malaria in North America, *American Journal of Tropical Medicine* 21: 223–44.

Capowski, G. 1996, The joy of flex, *American Management Association* 85: 12–18.

Carr-Saunders, A. M. 1964, *World population: Past growth and present trends*, Oxford: Oxford University Press, 1936, reprint ed., London: Frank Cass & Co.

Case, R. A. M., Coghill, C., Harley, J. L., and Pearson, J. T. 1962, *Chester Beatty Research Institute abridged serial life tables, England and Wales 1841–1960, Part 1*, London: Chester Beatty Research Institute.

Cavelaars, A. E., Kunst, A. E., Geurts, J. J., Crialesi, R., Grotvedt, L., Helmert, U., Lahelma, E., Lundberg, O., Mielck, A., Rasmussen, N. K., Regidor, E., Spuhler, T., and Mackenbach, J. P. 2000, Persistent variations in average height between countries and between socio-economic groups: An overview of 10 European countries, *Annals of Human Biology* 27: 407–21.

Chamla, M. C. 1983, L'évolution recente de la stature en Europe occidentale (Périod 1960–1980), *Bulletins et memoires de la Société d'Anthropologie de Paris*, t. 10, serie 13: 195–224.

Chandra, R. K. 1975, Antibody formation in first and second generation offspring of nutritionally deprived rats, *Science* 190: 289–90.

Chandra, R. K. 1992, Nutrition and immunoregulation. Significance for host resistance to tumors and infectious diseases in humans and rodents, *Journal of Nutrition* 122: 754–57.

Charlson, M., Szatrowski, T. P., Peterson, J., and Gold, J. 1994, Validation of a combined comorbidity index, *Journal of Clinical Epidemiology* 47: 1245–51.

Chen, L. C., Chowdhury, A. K. M. A., and Huffman, S. L. 1980, Anthropometric assessment of energy-protein malnutrition and subsequent risk of mortality among pre-school aged children, *American Journal of Clinical Nutrition* 33: 1836–45.

Chernichovsky, D. 2000, The public–private mix in the modern health care system – Concepts, issues, and policy options revisited, NBER Working Paper No. 7881, Cambridge, Mass.: National Bureau of Economic Research.

Cipolla, C. M. 1974, *The economic history of world population*, 6th ed., Harmondsworth, Middlesex: Penguin Books.

Cipolla, C. M. 1980, *Before the industrial revolution: European society and economy, 1000–1700*, 2d ed., New York: W. W. Norton.

Clark, J. G. D. 1961, *World prehistory: An outline*, Cambridge: Cambridge University Press.

Coale, A. J. and Demeny, P. 1966. *Regional model life tables and stable populations*, Princeton, N.J.: Princeton University Press.

Colquhoun, P. 1814, *Treatise on the wealth, power, and resources of the British Empire*, London: Joseph Mawmay.

Costa, D. L. 1993a, Height, wealth, and disease among the native-born in the rural, antebellum North, *Social Science History* 17: 355–83.

Costa, D. L. 1993b, Height, weight, wartime stress, and older age mortality: Evidence from the Union Army records, *Explorations in Economic History* 30: 424–49.

Costa, D. L. 1996, Health and labor force participation of older men, 1900–1991, *Journal of Economic History* 56: 62–89.

Costa, D. L. 1998, *The evolution of retirement: An American economic history*, Chicago: University of Chicago Press.

Costa, D. L. Forthcoming, The measure of man and older age mortality: Evidence from the Gould Sample, *Journal of Economic History*.

Costa, D. L. and Steckel, R. H. 1997, Long-term trends in health, welfare, and economic growth in the United States, in *Health and welfare during industrialization*, Steckel, R. H. and Floud, R. (eds.), pp. 47–89, Chicago: University of Chicago Press.

Cox, W. M. and Alm, R. 1998, Time well spent: The declining *real* cost of living in the United States, in *1997 Annual report*, pp. 2–25, Dallas: Federal Reserve Bank of Dallas.

Creswell, J. L., Egger, P., Fall, C. H. D., Osmond, C., Fraser, R. B., and Barker, D. J. P. 1997, Is the age of menopause determined in utero? *Early Human Development* 49: 143–48.

Cutler, D. M. and Meara, E. 1998. The medical costs of the young and old: A forty-year perspective, in *Frontiers in the economics of aging*, Wise, D. A. (ed.), pp. 215–42, Chicago: University of Chicago Press.

Dasgupta, P. 1993, *Inquiry into well-being and destitution*, Oxford: Clarendon Press.

Davey Smith, G., Hart, C., Upton, M., Hole, D., Gillis, C., Watt, G., and Hawthorne, V. 2000, Height and risk of death among men and women: Aetiological implications of associations with cardiorespiratory disease and cancer mortality, *Journal of Epidemiology and Community Health* 54: 97–103.

David, P. A. and Solar, P. 1977, A bicentenary contribution to the history of the cost of living in America, *Research in Economic History* 2: 1–80.

Davidson, C. 1982, *A woman's work is never done: A history of housework in the British Isles, 1650–1950*, London: Chatto and Windus.

Derry, T. K. and Williams, T. I. 1960, *A short history of technology*, London: Oxford University Press.

Doblhammer, G. and Vaupel, J. W. 2001, Life span depends on month of birth, *Science* 98: 2934–39.

Douglass, R. L. and Torres, R. E. 1994, Evaluation of a managed care program for the non-Medicaid urban poor, *Journal of Health Care for the Poor and Underserved* 5: 83–98.

Drukker, J. W. 1994, The tradition of anthropometric history in the Netherlands, Paper presented at the National Bureau of Economic Research, Cambridge, Mass., 11–12 July.

Drukker, J. W. and Tassenaar, V. 1997, Paradoxes of modernization and material wellbeing in the Netherlands during the 19th century, in *Health and welfare during industrialization*, Steckel, R. H. and Floud, R. (eds.), pp. 331–77, Chicago: University of Chicago Press.

Dublin, L. I. 1928, *Health and wealth: A survey of the economics of world health*, New York and London: Harper and Brothers.

Dublin, L. I. and Lotka, A. J. 1936, *Length of life: A study of the life table*, New York: Ronald Press.

Dublin, L. I., Lotka, A. J., and Spiegelman, M. 1949, *Length of life: A study of the life table*, rev. ed., New York: Ronald Press.

Duggan, M. 2000, Hospital ownership and public medical spending, *Quarterly Journal of Economics* 115: 1343–73.

Dupâquier, J. 1989, Demographic crises and subsistence crises in France, 1650–1725, in *Famine, disease and the social order in early modern society*, Walter, J. and Schofield, R. (eds.), pp. 189–99, Cambridge: Cambridge University Press.

Easterlin, R. A. 1975, Farm production and income in old and new areas at mid-century, in *Essays in nineteenth century economic history: The old Northwest*, Kingaman, D. C. and Vedder, R. K. (eds.), pp. 77–117, Athens: Ohio University Press.

Eckstein, Z., Schultz, T. P., and Wolpin, K. I. 1985, Short-run fluctuations in fertility and mortality in pre-industrial Sweden, *European Economic Review* 26: 297–317.

Ecob, R. and Davey Smith, G. 1999, Income and health: What is the nature of the relationship? *Social Science and Medicine* 48: 693–705.

Economic report of the President transmitted to the Congress, 2002, Washington, D.C.: U.S. Government Printing Office.

Economist, 2003, A voyage of discovery: Biotechnology may yet renew the pharmaceutical industry (in survey section: Climbing the helical staircase: A survey of biotechnology), 366, no. 8317: 7–9.

Edmondson, B. 1996, Who needs two cars? *American Demographics* 18, no. 12: 14–15.

Elo, I. T. and Preston, S. H. 1992, Effects of early-life conditions on adult mortality: A review, *Population Index* 58: 186–212.

Eveleth, P. B. and Tanner, J. M. 1976, *Worldwide variation in human growth*, Cambridge: Cambridge University Press.

Eveleth, P. B. and Tanner, J. M. 1990, *Worldwide variation in human growth*, 2d ed., Cambridge: Cambridge University Press.

Fagan, B. M. 1977, *People of the earth*, 2d ed., Boston: Little, Brown.

FAO 1996, *Sixth world food survey*, Rome: FAO.

FAO/WHO/UNU 1985, *Energy and protein requirements. Report of a joint FAO/WHO/UNU expert committee*, WHO Technical Report Series 724, Geneva: World Health Organization.

Federal Interagency Forum on Aging-Related Statistics 2000, *Older Americans 2000: Key indicators of well-being*, Washington, D.C.: U.S. Government Printing Office.

Feinstein, C. H. 1988, The rise and fall of the Williamson Curve, *Journal of Economic History* 48: 699–729.

Flinn, M. W. 1970, *British population growth, 1700–1850*, London: Macmillan.

Flinn, M. W. 1974, The stabilization of mortality in pre-industrial Western Europe, *Journal of European Economic History* 3: 285–318.

Flinn, M. W. 1981, *The European demographic system, 1500–1820*, Baltimore: Johns Hopkins University Press.

Floud, R. 1984a, The heights of Europeans since 1750: A new source for European economic history, NBER Working Paper No. 1318, Cambridge, Mass.: National Bureau of Economic Research.

Floud, R. 1984b, Measuring the transformation of European economies: Income, health and welfare, Mimeograph, Birkbeck College.

Floud, R. 1998, Height, weight and body mass of the British population since 1820. NBER Historical Paper 108.

Floud, R., Wachter, K. W., and Gregory, A. 1990, *Height, health, and history: Nutritional status in the United Kingdom, 1750–1980*, Cambridge: Cambridge University Press.

Fogel, R. W. 1986, Nutrition and the decline in mortality since 1700: Some preliminary findings, in *Long-term factors in American economic growth*, Engerman, S. L. and Gallman, R. E. (eds.), pp. 439–55, Chicago: University of Chicago Press.

Fogel, R. W. 1987, Biomedical approaches to the estimation and interpretation of secular trends in equity, morbidity, mortality, and labor productivity in Europe, 1750–1980, Typescript, Center for Population Economics, University of Chicago.

Fogel, R. W. 1989, *Without consent or contract*, vol. 1, New York: W. W. Norton.

Fogel, R. W. 1992, Second thoughts on the European escape from hunger: Famines, chronic malnutrition, and mortality rates, in Osmani (ed.), pp. 243–86.

Fogel, R. W. 1993, New sources and new techniques for the study of secular trends in nutritional status, health, mortality and the process of aging, *Historical Methods* 26: 5–43.

Fogel, R. W. 1994, Economic growth, population theory, and physiology: The bearing of long-term processes on the making of economic policy, *American Economic Review* 84: 369–95.

Fogel, R. W. 1997, New findings on secular trends in nutrition and mortality: Some implications for population theory, in *Handbook of population and family economics*, vol. 1A, Rosenzweig, M. R. and Stark, O. (eds.), pp. 435–86, Amsterdam: Elsevier.

Fogel, R. W. 1999, Aspects of economic growth: A comparison of the U.S. and China, presented at the International Conference on Labor Markets and Unemployment Policy in Transitional China, 3–4 July 1999, Chengdu, Sichuan, China.

Fogel, R. W. 2000, *The fourth great awakening and the future of egalitarianism*, Chicago: University of Chicago Press.

Fogel, R. W. 2003, Changes in the process of aging during the twentieth century: Findings and procedures of the *Early Indicators* Project, NBER Working Paper No. 9941.

Fogel, R. W., Costa, D. L., and Kim, J. M. 1993, Secular trends in the distribution of chronic conditions and disabilities at young adult and late ages, 1860–1988: Some preliminary findings, Paper presented at the NBER Summer Institute, Economics of Aging Program, Cambridge, Mass.

Fogel, R. W. and Engerman, S. L. 1971, The economics of slavery, in *The reinterpretation of American economic history*, Fogel, R. W. and Engerman, S. L. (eds.), pp. 311–41, New York: Harper & Row.

Fogel, R. W., Floud, R., and Harris, B. (n.d.), A treatise on technophysio evolution and consumption. In progress.

Forsén, T., Ericksson, J. G., Tuomilehto, J., Teramo, K., Osmond, C., and Barker, D. J. 1997, Mother's weight in pregnancy and coronary heart disease in a cohort of Finnish men: Follow-up study, *British Medical Journal* 315: 837–40.

Fraker, P. J., Gershwin, M. E., Good, R. A., and Prasad, A. 1986, Interrelationships between zinc and immune function, *Federation Proceedings* 45: 1474–79.

Frankel, S., Elmwood, P., Sweetnam, P., Yarnell, J., and Davey Smith, G. 1996, Birthweight, body-mass index in middle age, and incident coronary heart disease, *Lancet* 348: 1478–80.

Freeman, H. E., Aiken, L. H., Blendon, R. J., and Corey, C. R. 1990, Uninsured working-age adults: Characteristics and consequences, *Health Services Research* 24: 811–23.

Freeman, H. E. and Corey, C. R. 1993, Insurance status and access to health services among poor persons, *Health Services Research* 28: 531–41.

Fridlizius, G. 1979, Sweden, in *European demography and economic growth*, Lee, W. R. (ed.), pp. 340–405, London: Croom Helm.

Fridlizius, G. 1984, The mortality decline in the first phase of the demographic transition: Swedish experiences, in *Pre-industrial population change*, Bengtsson, T., Fridlizius, G., and Ohlsson, R. (eds.), pp. 71–117, Stockholm: Almquist and Wiksell.

Friedman, G. C. 1982, The heights of slaves in Trinidad, *Social Science History* 6: 482–515.

Fries, J. F. 1980, Ageing, natural death, and the compression of morbidity, *New England Journal of Medicine* 303: 130–36.

Fries, J. F. 1990, The sunny side of aging, *JAMA: Journal of the American Medical Association* 263: 2354–55.

Fronstin, P. 2000, The working uninsured: Who they are, how they have changed, and the consequences of being uninsured – with presidential candidate proposal outlines, *EBRI Issue Brief* 224: 1–23.

Gallman, R. E. 1972, The pace and pattern of American economic growth, in *American economic growth: An economist's history of the United States*, Davis, L. E., Easterlin, R. A., and Parker, W. N. (eds.), pp. 15–60, New York: Harper & Row.

Gallman, R. E. and Wallis, J. J. (eds.) 1992, *American economic growth and standards of living before the Civil War*, Chicago: University of Chicago Press.

Galloway, P. R. 1986, Differentials in demographic responses to annual price variations in pre-revolutionary France: A comparison of rich and poor areas in Rouen, 1681–1787, *European Journal of Population* 2: 269–305.

Garrow, J. S., James, W. P. T., and Ralph, A. 2000, *Human nutrition and dietetics*, 10th ed., Edinburgh: Churchill Livingstone.

Gille, H. 1949, The demographic history of northern European countries in the eighteenth century, *Population Studies* 3: 3–70.

Goldin, C. 1990, *Understanding the gender gap: An economic history of American women*, New York: Oxford University Press.

Goubert, P. 1965, Recent theories and research in French population between 1500 and 1700, in *Population in history: Essays in historical demography*, Glass, D. V. and Eversley, D. E. C. (eds.), pp. 457–73, Chicago: Aldine.

Goubert, P. 1984, Public hygiene and mortality decline in France in the 19th century, in *Pre-industrial population change*, Bengtsson, T., Fridlizius, G., and Ohlsson, R. (eds.), pp. 151–59, Stockholm: Almquist and Wiksell.

Gould, B. A. 1869, *Investigations in the military and anthropological statistics of American soldiers*, New York: Hurd and Houghton.

Graham, E. and Crossen, C. 1996, The overloaded American: Too many things to do, too little time to do them, *Wall Street Journal*, March 8: R1.

Grantham, G. W. 1993, Divisions of labour: Agricultural productivity and occupational specialization in pre-industrial France, *Economic History Review* 46: 478–502.

Haines, M. R. 1979, The use of model life tables to estimate mortality for the United States in the late nineteenth century, *Demography* 16: 289–312.

Hannon, J. U. 1984a, The generosity of antebellum poor relief, *Journal of Economic History* 44: 810–21.

Hannon, J. U. 1984b, Poverty in the antebellum northeast: The view from New York State's poor relief rolls, *Journal of Economic History* 44: 1007–32.

Hannon, J. U. 1985, Poor relief policy in antebellum New York State: The rise and decline of the poorhouse, *Explorations in Economic History* 22: 233–56.

Harris, B. 2002, Public health, nutrition and the decline of mortality: The McKeown thesis revisited, Prepared for the conference Thomas McKeown: His Life and Work, held by the Centre for the History of Medicine, School of Medicine, University of Birmingham, and held at the Postgraduate Medical Centre, Queen Elizabeth Hospital, Birmingham, 21 September 2002.

Hattersley, L. 1999, Trends in life expectancy by social class – an update, *Health Statistics Quarterly* 02: 16–24.

Helleiner, K. F. 1967, The population of Europe from the Black Death to the eve of vital revolution, in *The Cambridge economic history of Europe*, vol. 4, *The economy of expanding Europe in the sixteenth and seventeenth centuries*, Rich, E. E. and Wilson, C. H. (eds.), pp. 1–95, Cambridge: Cambridge University Press.

Helmchen, L. 2003, Changes in the age at onset of chronic disease among elderly Americans, 1870–2000, Typescript, Center for Population Economics, University of Chicago.

Henry, J. A., Bolla, M., Osmond, C., Fall, C., Barker, D. J. P., and Humphries, S. E. 1997, The effects of genotype and infant weight on adult plasma levels of fibrinogen, factor VII, and LDL cholesterol are additive, *Journal of Medical Genetics* 34: 553–58.

Henry, L. 1965, The population in France in the eighteenth century, in *Population in history: Essays in historical demography*, Glass, D. V. and Eversley, D. E. C. (eds.), pp. 434–56, Chicago: Aldine.

Higgs, R. 1973, Mortality in rural America, 1870–1920: Estimates and conjectures, *Explorations in Economic History* 10: 177–95.

Higgs, R. 1979, Cycles and trends of mortality in eighteen large American cities, 1871–1900, *Explorations in Economic History* 16: 381–408.

Himmelfarb, G. 1983, *The idea of poverty: England in the early industrial age*, New York: Random House.

Hochschild, A. R. 1997, *The time bind: When work becomes home and home becomes work*, New York: Basic Books.

Holderness, B. A. 1989, Prices, productivity, and output, in *The agrarian history of England and Wales*, vol. 6, *1750–1850*, Mingay, G. E. (ed.), pp. 84–189, Cambridge: Cambridge University Press.

Hollingsworth, T. H. 1977, Mortality in the British peerage families since 1600, *Population* 32 (Numéro special): 323–52.

Hoskins, W. G. 1964, Harvest fluctuations and English economic history, 1480–1619, *Agricultural History Review* 12: 28–46.

Hoskins, W. G. 1968, Harvest fluctuations and English economic history, 1620–1759, *Agricultural History Review* 16: 15–31.

Hurst, J. 2000, Challenges for health systems in member countries of the Organisation for Economic Co-operation and Development, *Bulletin of the World Health Organization* 78: 751–60.

Hytten, F. E. and Leitch, I. 1971, *The physiology of human pregnancy*, 2d ed., Oxford: Blackwell Scientific.

INED. 1977, Sixième rapport sur la situation démographique de la France, *Population* 32: 253–338.

Iyer, S. N. 1993, Pension reform in developing countries, *International Labour Review* 132: 187–207.

Jacobzone, S. 2002. Healthy ageing and the challenges of new technologies: Can OECD social and health-care systems provide for the future? in *Biotechnology and healthy ageing: Policy implications of new research* (Proceedings of the OECD Workshop on Healthy Ageing and Biotechnology, 13–14 November 2000, Tokyo, Japan), pp. 37–53, Paris: OECD.

Jencks, C. 1994, *The homeless*, Cambridge, Mass.: Harvard University Press.

Kanjanapipatkul, T. 2001, The effect of month of birth on life span of Union Army Veterans, Typescript, Center for Population Economics, University of Chicago.

Karpinos, B. D. 1958, Height and weight of selective service registrants processed for military service during World War II, *Human Biology* 30: 292–321.

Kelley, A. C. and Williamson, J. G. 1983, What drives Third World city growth? Paper presented at the International Conference on the Economic Consequences of Population Change in Industrialized Countries, University of Paderborn, Paderborn, West Germany, 31 May–4 June 1983.

Keyfitz, N. and Flieger, W. 1968, *World population: An analysis of vital data*, Chicago: University of Chicago Press.

Keyfitz, N. and Flieger, W. 1990, *World population growth and aging: Demographic trends in the late twentieth century*, Chicago: University of Chicago Press.

Kielmann, A. A., DeSweemer, C., Chernichovsky, D., Uberoi, I. S., Masih, N., Taylor, C. E., Parker, R. L., Reinke, W. A., Kakar, N., and Sarma, R. S. S. 1983, *Child and maternal health in India: The Narangwal experiment*, Baltimore: Johns Hopkins University Press.

Kiil, V. 1939, *Stature and growth of Norwegian men during the past two hundred years*, Oslo: I Kommisjon hos. J. Dybwad.

Kim, J. M. 1993, Waaler surfaces: A new perspective on height, weight, morbidity, and mortality, Typescript, Center for Population Economics, University of Chicago.

Kim, J. M. 1995, The health of the elderly, 1990–2035: An alternative forecasting approach based on changes in human physiology, with implications for health care costs and policy, Typescript, Center for Population Economics, University of Chicago.

Kim, J. M. 1996, The economics of nutrition, body build, and health: Waaler surfaces and physical human capital, Ph.D. dissertation, University of Chicago.

Kiple, K. F. (ed.) 1993, *The Cambridge world history of human disease*, Cambridge: Cambridge University Press.

Komlos, J. 1989, Nutrition and economic development in the eighteenth-century Habsburg monarchy: An anthropometric history, Princeton, N.J.: Princeton University Press.

Kotlikoff, L. J. 1996, Privatizing Social Security: How it works and why it matters, in *Tax policy and the economy*, vol. 10, Poterba, J. (ed.), pp. 1–32, Cambridge, Mass.: MIT Press.

Koupilová, I., Leon, D. A., and Vågerö, D. 1997, Can confounding by sociodemographic and behavioural factors explain the association between size at birth and blood pressure at age 50 in Sweden? *Journal of Epidemiology and Community Health* 51: 14–18.

Kuh, D. and Davey Smith, G. 1993, When is mortality risk determined? Historical insights into a current debate, *Social History of Medicine* 6: 101–23.

Kunitz, S. J. 1983, Speculation on the European mortality decline, *Economic History Review* 36: 349–64.

Kunitz, S. J. 1986, Mortality since Malthus, in *The state of population theory: Forward from Malthus*, Coleman, D. and Schofield, R. (eds.), pp. 279–302, Oxford: Blackwell.

Kuznets, S. 1952, Long-term changes in the national income of the United States of America since 1870, in *Income and wealth of the United States: Trends and structure*, Kuznets, S. (ed.), pp. 29–241, Baltimore: Johns Hopkins University Press.

Kuznets, S. 1971, *Economic growth of nations: Total output and production structure*, Chicago: University of Chicago Press.

Landes, D. S. 1969, *The unbound Prometheus: Technological change and industrial development from 1750 to the present*, Cambridge: Cambridge University Press.

Landes, D. S. 1998, *The wealth and poverty of nations: Why some are so rich and some so poor*, New York: W. W. Norton.

Langer, W. L. 1975, American foods and Europe's population growth 1750–1850, *Journal of Social History* 8: 51–66.

Laslett, P. [1965] 1984, *The world we have lost: England before the industrial age*, 3d ed., New York: Charles Scribner's Sons.

Laslett, P. 1991, *A fresh map of life*, Cambridge, Mass.: Harvard University Press.

Law, C. M. and Shiell, A. W. 1996, Is blood pressure inversely related to birth weight? The strength of evidence from a systematic review of the literature, *Journal of Hypertension* 14: 935–41.

Lebrun, F. 1971, *Les hommes et la mort en Anjou aux 17e et 18e siècles*, Paris: Mouton Publishers.

Lee, C. 1995, Secular trends in LFPR of older males, 1890–1930, Typescript, Center for Population Economics, University of Chicago.

Lee, C. 1996, Essays on retirement and wealth accumulation in the United States, 1850–1990, Ph.D. dissertation, University of Chicago.

Lee, C. 2000. Appendix 5E, The relation of the growth in income inequality to the organization of work and the structure of consumption, in Fogel, R., *The fourth great awakening and the future of egalitarianism*, pp. 272–83, Chicago: University of Chicago Press.

Lee, R. 1981, Short-term variation: Vital rates, prices and weather, in Wrigley and Schofield, pp. 356–401, Oxford: Blackwell.

Lee, W. R. 1980, The mechanism of mortality change in Germany, 1750–1850, *Medizinhistorisches Journal* 15: 244–68.

Lee, W. R. 1984, Mortality levels and agrarian reforms in early 19th century Prussia: Some regional evidence, in *Pre-industrial population change*, Bengtsson, T., Fridlizius, G., and Ohlsson, R. (eds.), pp. 161–90, Stockholm: Almquist and Wiksell.

Lenk, H. 1994, Value changes and the achieving society: A social-philosophical perspective, in *OECD societies in transition: The future of work and leisure*, pp. 81–94, Paris: OECD.

Leon, D. A., Lithell, H. O., Vågerö, D., Koupilová, I., Mohsen, R., Berglund, L., Lithell, U.-B., and McKeigue, P. M. 1998, Reduced fetal growth rate and increased risk of death from ischaemic heart disease: Cohort study of 15,000 Swedish men and women born 1915–29, *British Medical Journal* 317: 241–45.

Linder, F. E. and Grove, R. D. 1947, *Vital statistics rates in the United States 1900–1940*, Washington, D.C.: U.S. Government Printing Office.

Lindert, P. H. 1986, Comment, in *Long-term factors in American economic growth*, Engerman, S. L. and Gallman, R. E. (eds.), pp. 527–37, Chicago: University of Chicago Press.

Lindert, P. H. and Williamson, J. G. 1982, Revising England's social tables: 1688–1812, *Explorations in Economic History* 19: 385–408.

Lindert, P. H. and Williamson, J. G. 1983, English workers' living standards during the industrial revolution: A new look, *Economic History Review* 36: 1–25.

Liu, Y., Hsaio, W. C., and Eggleston, K. 1999, Equity in health and health care: The Chinese experience, *Social Science and Medicine* 49: 1349–56.

Livi-Bacci, M. 1983, The nutrition–mortality link in past times: A comment, *Journal of Interdisciplinary History* 14: 293–98.

Livi-Bacci, M. 1991, *Population and nutrition: An essay on European demographic history*, New York: Cambridge University Press.

Lyall, S. 1999, Britain's prescription for health care: Take a seat, *New York Times*, 18 April, sec. 1, p. 3.

Maddison, A. 1991, *Dynamic forces in capitalist development*, Oxford: Oxford University Press.

Maddison, A. 1995, *Monitoring the world economy, 1820–1992*. Paris: OECD.

Maddison, A. 2001, *The world economy: A millennial perspective*. Paris: OECD.

Malmström, M., Sundquist, J., and Johansson, S.-E. 1999, Neighborhood environment and self-reported health status: A multi-level analysis, *American Journal of Public Health* 89: 1181–86.

Manton, K. G. 1993, Biomedical research and changing concepts of disease and aging: Implications for long-term forecasts for elderly populations, in *Forecasting the health of elderly populations*, Manton, K. G., Singer, B. H., and Suzman, R. M. (eds.), pp. 319–65, New York: Springer-Verlag.

Manton, K. G., Corder, L., and Stallard, E. 1997, Chronic disability trends in elderly United States populations: 1982–1994, *Proceedings of the National Academy of Sciences, USA* 96: 2593–98.

Manton, K. G. and Gu, X. 2001, Changes in the prevalence of chronic disability in the United States black and nonblack population above age 65 from 1982 to 1999, *Proceedings of the National Academy of Sciences, USA* 98: 6354–59.

Manton, K. G., Stallard, E., and Corder, L. 1997, Changes in the age dependence of mortality and disability: Cohort and other determinants, *Demography* 34: 135–57.

Marks, J. 1995, Time out, *U.S. News and World Report* 11 Dec.: 85–96.

Martorell, R. 1985, Child growth retardation: A discussion of its causes and its relationship to health, in *Nutritional adaptation in man*, Blaxter, K. and Waterlow, J. C. (eds.), pp. 13–30, London: John Libbey.

May, J. M. 1958, *The ecology of human disease*, New York: MD Publishing.

Mayr, E. 1982, *The growth of biological thought: Diversity, evolution, and inheritance*, Cambridge, Mass.: Belknap Press.

McCutcheon, B. J. 1992, An exploration into the courses of the growth of per capita income in the North, 1840–1860, in *Without consent or contract*, vol. 2, *Evidence and methods*, Fogel, R. W., Galantine, R. A., and Manning, R. L. (eds.), pp. 485–96, New York: W. W. Norton.

McKeown, T. 1976, *The modern rise of population*, New York: Academic Press.

McKeown, T. 1978, Fertility, mortality and cause of death: An examination of issues related to the modern rise of population, *Population Studies* 32: 535–42.

McKeown, T. 1979, *The role of medicine: Dream, mirage, or nemesis?* Princeton, N.J.: Princeton University Press.

McNeill, W. 1971, *A world history*, 2d ed., New York: Oxford University Press.

Meeker, E. 1972, The improving of health of the United States, 1850–1915, *Explorations in Economic History* 9: 353–73.

Meinhold, H., Campos-Barros, A., Walzog, B., Köhler, R., Müller, F., and Behne, D. 1993, Effects of selenium and iodine deficiency on type I, type II and type III iodothyronine deiodinases and circulating thyroid hormones in the rat, *Experimental and Clinical Endocrinology* 101(2): 87–93.

Meuvret, J. 1946, Les crises de subsistances et la demographie de la France d'ancien régime, *Population* 1: 643–50.

Meuvret, J. 1965, Demographic crisis in France from the sixteenth to the eighteenth century, in *Population in history: Essays in historical demography*, Glass, D. V. and Eversley, D. E. C. (eds.), pp. 507–22, Chicago: Aldine.

Michelozzi, P., Perucci, C. A., Forastiere, F., Fusco, D., Ancona, C., and Dell'Orca, V. 1999, Inequality in health: Socioeconomic differentials in mortality in Rome, 1990–95, *Journal of Epidemiology and Community Health* 53: 687–93.

Mitchison, R. 1977, *British population change since 1860*, New York: Macmillan.

Moffit, R. 1968–92, Current population surveys: March individual level extract, 1968–1992, Inter-University Consortium for Political and Social Research #6171.

Murray, C. J. L. and Lopez, A. D. (eds.) 1996, *The global burden of disease: A comprehensive assessment of mortality and disability from diseases, injuries, and risk factors in 1990 and projected to 2020*, Cambridge: Harvard School of Public Health for The World Health Organization and The World Bank.

New York City Department of Health 1871, *First annual report of the Board of Health of the Health Department of the City of New York, April 11, 1870, to April 10, 1871*, New York: New York Printing Co., 1871.

New York State Board of Health 1867, *Annual report*, Albany, N.Y.: Van Benthuysen.

Newhouse, J. P. 2001, Medicare policy in the 1990s, NBER Working Paper No. 8531.

Oddy, D. J. 1990, Food, drink and nutrition, in *The Cambridge social history of Britain 1750–1950*, vol. 2, *People and their environment*, Thompson, F. M. L. (ed.), pp. 251–78, New York: Cambridge University Press.

Oeppen, J. and Vaupel, J. W. 2002, Broken limits to life expectancy, *Science* 296: 1029–31.

Oeppen, J. and Vaupel, J. W. 2002 suppl., Broken limits to life expectancy, supplementary material. Available on the Internet at http://www.sciencemag.org/cgi/content/full/296/5570/1029/DC1 (last accessed 29 July 2003).

Organization for Economic Co-operation and Development 2001, *Society at a glance: OECD social indicators*, 2001 ed., Paris: OECD.

Orr, J. B. 1936. *Food, health and income. Report on a survey of adequacy of diet in relation to income*. London: Macmillan.

Osmani, S. R. 1992a, On some controversies in the measurement of undernutrition, in Osmani (ed.), pp. 121–64.

Osmani, S. R. (ed.) 1992b, *Nutrition and poverty*, Oxford: Oxford University Press.

Paneth, N. and Susser, M. 1995, Early origin of coronary heart disease (the 'Barker Hypothesis'), *British Medical Journal* 310: 411–12.

Pappas, G., Queen, S., Hadden, W., and Fisher, G. 1993, The increasing disparity in mortality between socioeconomic groups in the United States, 1960 and 1986, *New England Journal of Medicine* 329: 103–9.

Peak, M. H. 1996, Face-time follies, *Management Review* 85: 1.

Perkin, H. J. 1990, *The rise of professional society: England since 1880*, London and New York: Routledge.

Perrenoud, A. 1984, Mortality decline in its secular setting, in *Pre-industrial population change*, Bengtsson, T., Fridlizius, G., and Ohlsson, R. (eds.), pp. 41–69, Stockholm: Almquist and Wiksell.

Perry, C. W. and Rosen, H. S. 2001. Insurance and the utilization of medical services among the self-employed, NBER Working Paper No. 8490, Cambridge, Mass.: National Bureau of Economic Research.

Perry, I. J., Beevers, D. G., Whincup, P. H., and Bareford, D. 1995, Predictors of ratio of placental weight to fetal weight in multiethnic community, *British Medical Journal* 310: 436–39.

Phelps Brown, H. 1988, *Egalitarianism and the generation of inequality*, New York: Oxford University Press.

Piggott, S. 1965, *Ancient Europe from the beginnings of agriculture to classical antiquity*, Chicago: Aldine.

Pollard, S. 1981, Sheffield and sweet Auburn – amenities and living standards in the British industrial revolution, *Journal of Economic History* 41: 902–4.

Poortvliet, W. G. and Laine, T. P. 1995, A global trend: Privatization and reform of social security pension plans, *Benefits Quarterly* 11: 63–84.

Preston, S. H. 1975, The changing relation between mortality and level of economic development, *Population Studies* 29: 231–48.

Preston, S. H. 1985, Resources, knowledge, and child mortality: A comparison of the U.S. in the late nineteenth century and developing countries today, in *International Population Conference, Florence, 5–12 June*, vol. 2, pp. 373–86, Liège, Belgium: International Union for the Scientific Study of Population.

Preston, S. H., Keyfitz, N., and Schoen, R. 1972, *Causes of death: Life tables for national populations*, New York: Seminar Press.

Preston, S. H. and van de Walle, E. 1978, Urban French mortality in the nineteenth century, *Population Studies* 32: 275–97.

Quenouille, M. H., Boyne, A. W., Fisher, W. B., and Leitch, I. 1951, Statistical studies of recorded energy expenditure in man, Technical Communication no. 17, Aberdeenshire, Scotland: Commonwealth Bureau of Animal Nutrition.

Raper, N. R., Zizza, C., and Rourke, J. 1992, *Nutritional content of the U.S. food supply, 1909–1988*, U.S. Department of Agriculture Home Economics Research Report no. 50, Washington, D.C.: U.S. Department of Agriculture.

Ravelli, A. C. J., van der Meulen, J. H. P., Michels, R. P. J., Osmond, C., Barker, D. J. P., Hales, C. N., and Bleker, O. P. 1998, Glucose tolerance in adults after prenatal exposure to famine, *Lancet* 351: 173–77.

Razzell, P. E. 1973, An interpretation of the modern rise of population in Europe – A critique, *Population Studies* 28: 5–170.

Rebaudo, D. 1979, Le mouvement annuel de la population française rurale de 1670 à 1740, *Population* 34: 589–606.

Richards, R. J. 1992, Evolution, in *Keywords in evolutionary biology*, Keller, E. F. and Lloyd, E. A. (eds.), pp. 95–105, Cambridge, Mass.: Harvard University Press.

Richards, T. 1984, Weather, nutrition and the economy: The analysis of short run fluctuations in births, deaths and marriages, France 1740–1909, in *Pre-industrial population change*, Bengtsson, T., Fridlizius, G., and Ohlsson, R. (eds.), pp. 357–89, Stockholm: Almquist and Wiksell International.

Rifkin, J. 1995, *The end of work: The decline of the global labor force and the dawn of the post-market era*, New York: G. P. Putnam's Sons.

Robinson, J. P. 1988, Who's doing the housework? *American Demographics* 10, no. 12: 24–28, 63.

Robinson, J. P. and Godbey, G. 1997, *Time for life: The surprising ways Americans use their time*, University Park: Pennsylvania State University Press.

Roede, M. J. and van Wieringen, J. C. 1985, Growth diagrams, 1980, *Tijdschrift voor Sociale Gezondheidszorg* 63(suppl.): 62–68.

Rolland-Cachera, M. F., Cole, T. J., Sempe, M., Tichet, J., Rossignol, C., and Charraud, A. 1991, Body Mass Index variations: Centiles from birth to 87 years, *European Journal of Clinical Nutrition* 45: 13–21.

Rona, R. J., Swan, A. V., and Altman, D. G. 1978, Social factors and height of primary schoolchildren in England and Wales, *Journal of Epidemiology and Community Health* 32: 147–54.

Sandberg, L. G. and Steckel, R. H. 1987, Heights and economic history: The Swedish case, *Annals of Human Biology* 14: 101–10.

Schmidt, I. M., Jorgensen, M. H., and Michaelsen, K. F. 1995, Height of conscripts in Europe: Is postneonatal mortality a predictor? *Annals of Human Biology* 22: 57–67.

Schoeller, D. A. 1990, How accurate is self-reported dietary energy intake? *Nutrition Reviews* 48: 373–79.

Schor, J. 1991, *The overworked American: The unexpected decline of leisure*, New York: Basic Books.

Schuller, A. 1999, Better oral health, more inequality, *Community Dental Health* 16: 154–59.

Scott, M. B. 1996, Work/life programs encompass broad range of benefit offerings, *Employee Benefit Plan Review* 51: 26–31.

Scrimshaw, N. S. 1997, More evidence that foetal nutrition contributes to chronic disease in later life, *British Medical Journal* 315: 825–26.

Scrimshaw, N. S. and Gordon, J. E. (eds.) 1968, *Malnutrition, learning and behavior*, Cambridge, Mass.: MIT Press.

Scrimshaw, N. S., Taylor, C. E., and Gordon, J. E. 1968, *Interactions of nutrition and infection*, Geneva: World Health Organization.

Sekhri, N. K. 2000, Managed care: The U.S. experience, *Bulletin of the World Health Organization* 78: 830–44.

Sen, A. 1981, *Poverty and famines: An essay on entitlement and deprivation*, Oxford: Clarendon Press.

Shah-Canning, D., Alpert, J. J., and Bauchner, H. 1996, Care-seeking patterns of inner-city families using an emergency room. A three-decade comparison, *Medical Care* 34: 1171–79.

Shammas, C. 1990, *The pre-industrial consumer in England and America*, Oxford: Clarendon Press.

Shaw, G. B. [1928] 1931, *The intelligent woman's guide to socialism and capitalism. The collected works of George Bernard Shaw*, vol. 20, Ayot St. Lawrence edition, New York: Wm. H. Wise.

Shellenbarger, S. 1997, New job hunters ask recruiters, 'is there a life after work?' *Wall Street Journal*, 29 Jan.: B1.

Singer, B. H. and Manton, K. G. 1998. The effects of health changes on projections of health service needs for the elderly population, *Proceedings of the National Academy of Sciences, USA* 95: 15618–22.

Slicher van Bath, B. H. 1963, *The agrarian history of Western Europe A.D. 500–1850*, Ordish, O. (trans.), London: Edward Arnold.

Smillie, W. G. 1955, *Public health: Its promise for the future*, New York: Macmillan.

Smith, D. S. 1977, A homeostatic demographic regime: Patterns in West European family reconstitution studies, in *Population patterns in the past*, Lee, R. D. (ed.), pp. 19–51, New York: Academic Press.

Soltow, L. 1968, Long-run changes in British income inequality, *Economic History Review* 21: 17–29.

Sommer, A. and Lowenstein, M. S. 1975, Nutritional status and mortality: A prospective validation of the QUAC stick, *American Journal of Clinical Nutrition* 28: 287–92.

Srinivasan, T. N. 1992, Undernutrition: Concepts, measurement, and policy implications, in Osmani (ed.), pp. 97–120.

Statistical yearbook of China 2001, 2001, Beijing: China Statistical Publishing House.

Steckel, R. H. 1995, Stature and the standard of living, *Journal of Economic Literature* 33: 1903–40.

Stein, C. E., Fall, C. H., Kumaran, K., Osmond, C., Cox, V., and Barker, D. J. 1996, Fetal growth and coronary heart disease in South India, *Lancet* 348: 1269–73.

Stein, C. E., Kumaran, K., Fall, C. H., Shaheen, S. O., Osmond, C., and Barker, D. J. 1997, Relation of fetal growth to adult lung function in South India, *Thorax* 52: 895–99.

Stolnitz, G. 1955, A century of international mortality trends: I, *Population Studies* 9: 24–55.

Stolnitz, G. 1956, A century of international mortality trends: II, *Population Studies* 10: 17–42.

Stuck, A. E., Walthert, J. M., Nikolaus, T., Bula, C. J., Hohmann, C., and Beck, J. C. 1999, Risk factors for functional status decline in community-living elderly people: A systematic literature review, *Social Science & Medicine* 48: 445–69.

Sukhatme, P. V. (ed.) 1982, *Newer concepts in nutrition and their implications for policy*, Pune, India: Maharastra Association for the Cultivation of Science Research Institute.

Tanner, J. M. 1982, The potential of auxological data for monitoring economic and social well-being, *Social Science History* 6: 571–81.

Tanner, J. M. 1990, *Foetus into man: Physical growth from conception to maturity*, rev. ed., Cambridge, Mass.: Harvard University Press.

Tanner, J. M. 1993, Review of *fetal and infant origins of adult disease*, ed. D. J. P. Barker, *Annals of Human Biology* 20: 508–9.

Toutain, J. 1971, La consommation alimentaire en France de 1789 à 1964, *Economies et Sociétés, Cahiers de l'ISEA* 5: 1909–2049.

Trewartha, G. T. 1969, *A geography of populations: World patterns*, New York: John Wiley & Sons.

Tüchsen, F. and Endahl, L. A. 1999, Increasing inequality in ischaemic heart disease morbidity among employed men in Denmark, *International Journal of Epidemiology* 28: 640–44.

United Nations 1953, *The determinants and consequences of population trends*, New York: United Nations.

United Nations 1973, *Determinants and consequences of population trends: New summary of findings on interaction of demographic, economic and social factors*, New York: United Nations.

United Nations 1990, *Human development report 1990*, New York: Oxford University Press.

U.S. Bureau of the Census 1975, *Historical statistics of the United States, colonial times to 1970*, Washington, D.C.: U.S. Government Printing Office.

U.S. Bureau of the Census 1994, Current population survey: Annual demographic file, 1994 [Computer File], Washington, D.C.: U.S. Department of Commerce, Bureau of the Census [producer]; Ann Arbor, Mich.: Inter-university Consortium for Political and Social Research [distributor], 1995 (#6461).

U.S. Bureau of the Census 1996, *Statistical abstract of the United States*, 116th ed., Washington, D.C.: U.S. Bureau of the Census.

U.S. Census Bureau 2000a, *Statistical abstract of the United States*, 120th ed., Washington, D.C.: U.S. Bureau of the Census.

U.S. Census Bureau 2000b, Table C, Projected life expectancy at birth by race and Hispanic origin, 1999 to 2100. Available on the Internet at http://www.census.gov/population/documentation/twps0038/tabC.txt (last accessed 29 July 2003).

U.S. Department of Labor, Bureau of Labor Statistics 1994, Consumer expenditure survey, 1994: Interview survey and detailed expediture files [Computer File], ICPSP Version, Washington, D.C.: U.S. Department of Labor, Bureau of Labor Statistics [producer], 1996; Ann Arbor, Mich.: Inter-university Consortium for Political and Social Research [distributor], 1997 (#6710).

U.S. Department of Labor Statistics 1959, *How American buying habits change*, Washington, D.C.: U.S. Government Printing Office.

U.S. National Center for Health Statistics 1997, *Monthly Vital Statistics Report* 46, no. 1, suppl. (11 Sept.).

U.S. Public Health Service 1963, *Vital statistics of the United States 1960*, Washington, D.C.: U.S. Government Printing Office.

U.S. Social Security Administration 1997, *Annual report*, Washington, D.C.: U.S. Government Printing Office.

Usher, D. 1973, An imputation to the measure of economic growth for changes in life expectancy, in *The measurement of economic and social performance*, Moss, M. (ed.), pp. 193–226, New York: National Bureau of Economic Research (distributed by Columbia University Press).

Usher, D. 1980, *The measurement of economic growth*, New York: Columbia University Press.

Utterström, G. 1965, Two essays on population in eighteenth-century Scandinavia, in *Population in history: Essays in historical demography*, Glass, D. V. and Eversley, D. E. C. (eds.), pp. 523–48, Chicago: Aldine.

van Poppel, F. and van der Heijden, C. 1997, The effects of water supply on infant and childhood mortality: A review of historical evidence, *Health Transition Review: The Cultural, Social, and Behavioural Determinants of Health* 7: 113–48.

van Wieringen, J. C. 1986, Secular growth changes. In *Human growth: A comprehensive treatise*, vol. 3, *Methodology. Ecological, genetic, and nutritional effects on growth*, Falkner, F. and Tanner, J. M. (eds.), 2d ed., pp. 307–71, New York: Plenum Press.

Veblen, T. [1899] 1934, *The theory of the leisure class: An economic study of institutions*, New York: Modern Library.

Von Meerton, M. A. 1989, Croissance économique en France et accroissement des français: Une analyse "Villermetrique," Typescript, Center voor Economische Studiën, Leuven.

Waaler, H. T. 1984, Height, weight and mortality: The Norwegian experience, *Acta Medica Scandinavica* suppl. 679: 1–51.

Wallihan, D. B., Stump, T. E., and Callahan, C. M. 1999, Accuracy of self-reported health service use and patterns of care among urban older adults, *Medical Care* 37: 662–70.

Warren, C. 2000, *Brush with death: A social history of lead poisoning*, Baltimore: Johns Hopkins University Press.

Waterlow, J. C., Tomkins, A. M., and Grantham-McGregor, S. M. 1992, *Protein energy malnutrition*, London: Edward Arnold.

Weir, D. R. 1982, Fertility transition in rural France, 1740–1829, Ph.D. dissertation, Stanford University.

Weir, D. R. 1989, Markets and mortality in France, 1600–1879, in *Famine, disease and the social order in early modern society*, Walter, J. and Schofield, R. (eds.), pp. 201–34, Cambridge: Cambridge University Press.

Weir, D. R. 1993, Parental consumption decisions and child health during the early French fertility decline, 1790–1914, *Journal of Economic History* 53: 259–74.

Williamson, J. G. 1976, American prices and urban inequality since 1820, *Journal of Economic History* 36: 303–33.

Williamson, J. G. 1981a, Urban disamenities, dark satanic mills, and the British standard of living debate, *Journal of Economic History* 41: 75–83.

Williamson, J. G. 1981b, Some myths die hard – urban disamenities one more time: A reply, *Journal of Economic History* 41: 905–7.

Williamson, J. G. 1982, Was the industrial revolution worth it? Disamenities and death in 19th century British towns, *Explorations in Economic History* 19: 221–45.

Williamson, J. G. 1984, British mortality and the value of life, 1781–1931, *Population Studies* 38: 157–72.

Williamson, J. G. 1985, *Did British capitalism breed inequality?* Boston: Allen & Unwin.

Williamson, J. G. and Lindert, P. H. 1980, *American inequality: A microeconomic history*, New York: Academic Press.

Winter, J. M. 1982, The decline of mortality in Britain 1850–1980. In *Population and society in Britain 1850–1980*, Barker, T. and Drake, M. (eds.), pp. 100–20, New York: New York University Press.

World Bank 1990, *World development report 1990*, New York: Oxford University Press.

World Bank 1992, *World development report 1992*, New York: Oxford University Press.

World Bank 1993, *The East Asian miracle: Economic growth and public policy*, New York: Oxford University Press.

World Bank 1997, *World development report 1997: The state in a changing world*, New York: Oxford University Press.

World Bank 2001, *World development report 2000/2001: Attacking poverty*, New York: Oxford University Press.

World Health Organization 2000, *The world health report 2000. Health systems: Improving performance*, Geneva: World Health Organization.

World Health Organization, Commission on Macroeconomics and Health 2001, *Macroeconomics and Health: Investing in Health for Economic Development*, Report of the Commission on Macroeconomics and Health, Geneva: World Health Organization.

World Health Organization, Regional Office for Europe 1997, Highlights on health in the United Kingdom (draft), European Communities and WHO, April 1997. Available on the Internet at http://www.euro.who.int/document/e62043.pdf (last accessed 2 February 2003).

Wrigley, E. A. 1969, *Population and history*, London: Weidenfeldt and Nicolson.

Wrigley, E. A. 1987, Urban growth and agricultural change: England and the Continent in the early modern period, in *People, cities and wealth: The transformation of traditional society*, pp. 157–93, Oxford: Blackwell.

Wrigley, E. A. and Schofield, R. S. 1981, *The population history of England, 1541–1871: A reconstruction*, Oxford: Blackwell.

Index

Cambridge Studies in Population, Economy
and Society in Past Time